You and Your Feelings

You and Your Feelings

by Eda LeShan

MACMILLAN PUBLISHING CO., INC.
New York
COLLIER MACMILLAN PUBLISHERS
London

Macmillan Publishing Co., Inc.
866 Third Avenue, New York, N.Y. 10022
Collier-Macmillan Canada Ltd.

Printed in the United States of America

1   2   3   4   5   6   7   8   9   10

Library of Congress Cataloging in Publication Data
LeShan, Eda J   You and your feelings.
1. Adolescent psychology—Juvenile literature.
2. Emotions—Juvenile literature.   [1. Adolescence.
2. Emotions]   I. Title.
BF724.3.E5L47   155.5   74-22254
ISBN 0-02-757330-3

Many years ago my mother, Jean Schick Grossman, wrote with sensitive compassion and understanding about teenagers. This book is dedicated to her in loving memory and the hope I learned enough to pass it on.

ACKNOWLEDGMENTS
I would like to express my grateful appreciation to all the young people who were willing to discuss this book with me, who wrote letters and compositions in order to help me understand their feelings. My very special thanks to teachers Ms. Joan Price and Ms. Christine Strano, and to their students in the Richmond Unified School District, Richmond, California, who provided me with a wealth of wonderful material. Thanks also to Mrs. Sadie Hofstein and Mrs. Dorothy Gunzenhauser for providing me with reference materials, and to Lee Polk and Dr. Florence Miale for reading the manuscript. My love and gratitude also to my daughter, Wendy, who taught me most of all about what it means to grow up in today's world, and to my husband, Lawrence LeShan, for his support and encouragement in all my undertakings.

Contents

You and Your Feelings

1
You and Your Feelings

I scream
I scream loud
I scream with hate, anger and love
 all mixed up together
I scream with confusion
I scream with fright
I cry with no reason at all
Everything builds up inside me
 until I open up
Let everything out
I SCREAM, CRY, YELL, CURSE, HIT AND
 close up again
Until there's another time when I let
 everything out

By Angela Powlen, 1971

1

Do you think something is wrong with Angela? Does she seem unusually emotional or disturbed? She's not; there is nothing at all abnormal about her—she was just eleven and one-half years old when she wrote that poem.

If you are a young person between twelve and sixteen years of age, I think you can understand how Angela felt. You feel this is the hardest time of your whole life—and you are right! Some of your parents and teachers have probably told you that these are the best years of your life. Maybe some of you have believed them, even though you are hurting much of the time.

When I began to write this book and asked young people to tell me about their feelings, here are some of the things they said:

"The worst thing is, who am I and why does everyone think I'm somebody I'm not?"

"Why am I so ugly, gawky, stupid, depressed, shy, bored, and silly?"

"I never know how I'm going to feel in the next minute."

"I can't stand looking at myself in the mirror, because I seem to hate the face I see."

"Everybody who tells me they love me—I really feel they hate me."

"Even when I'm smiling and joking, I'm really crying inside."

Why is this a time when young people feel happy and depressed, loving and hating, quiet and excited—

2

all mixed up together? Why is this such a difficult time of life? There are some very good reasons. There are probably two kinds of feelings that are most noticeable between the ages of twelve and sixteen: rapid changes in mood and great self-consciousness. Thirteen-year-old Karen* says, "I can be crying like crazy one minute and then maybe something nice happens and I think I'm the happiest person alive." Joe, age fourteen, says, "I am so self-conscious that I'm afraid to go to the front of the room to sharpen a pencil. Whenever anything happens that I attract attention, I can feel myself begin to blush. The quicker I can get away the better I like it."

The most significant reason for these feelings is that you are going through the most dramatic physical changes that will ever occur in your lifetime. You are changing from having the body of a child to that of an adult. During the years that this remarkable and scary process is taking place, glands in your body begin to secrete hormones that bring about this growth and change; but in addition to affecting the way you look, they also affect the way you feel.

Feelings of sadness and fear, of being way down in the dumps or up in the clouds, are due in part to the effects of physical, glandular changes. These are feelings that are very hard to change, but it helps somewhat when you understand that they are normal and will pass. A young woman who is now eighteen was reminiscing about how she felt when she was about

* All names are fictitious.

3

thirteen or fourteen and she told me, "I had a wonderful physical education teacher who said you had to treat your feelings as if they were ocean waves, rolling into shore, disappearing, then a new one rolling along. She said we should imagine that we are either sitting on the beach watching the waves or floating right on them; just to let them happen, knowing they would keep coming and going and changing. That image inside my head helped a lot. I knew I couldn't do anything about these waves of feeling so I just let them happen."

Of course many feelings have more to do with what is happening to us in our daily lives, and they will be talked about throughout this book. These are the kinds of feelings that we can do a great deal to understand and to change.

The universal and awful feelings of shyness and self-consciousness are quite understandable when you think about what is happening to the adolescent's body. Arms are getting longer, feet are getting bigger, girls' legs begin to have a more rounded shape, and boys' legs seem to get skinnier and wobbly, moving in too many directions at once. Parts of the body get fatter, parts get thinner; hair begins to appear under arms, on the chests and faces of boys, and in the genital area of both sexes. Girls' breasts begin to take completely new and widely differing sizes and shapes, and boys become aware of changes in their genitals. Suddenly it seems that everybody in the class is too tall or too short, too skinny or too fat! And at the very moment when a young person is suffering from a greater lack of self-confidence than he may ever experience again, he may also develop acne, which adds to the other physical woes. Sixty-five percent of teenage girls and 59 percent of boys develop acne.

You find yourself living inside the body of a stranger; a body that seems to change from day to day; a body that seems to you to be terribly different from every other body you see around you. And worst of all, you have absolutely no way of knowing how it is going to turn out—whether you will be tall or short, hairy or not so hairy, and of course girls have no way of knowing if they will end up looking like Twiggy or Raquel Welch. The feeling that comes naturally under such circumstances is to hate one's own body, to feel ashamed of it.

One of the things that makes it more difficult to endure bodily changes while they are going on is that many young people tend to confuse the word "average" with the word "normal." While it may be true that the average height of women might by 5'5", it is still perfectly normal for a woman to be 4'9" or 6 feet tall. Every research study done on adolescence has confirmed the fact that there are great variations within the normal range of development. It is normal to start menstruating at ten or at sixteen; it is normal to develop body hair at twelve or fifteen. It is normal for a boy's voice to change at eleven or seventeen. It is normal for a girl to need a size 30 or a size 38 bra. Laura, age twelve, commented, "It seems to me nobody in my class is average!" She's right. An average is just a statistical figure arrived at by adding up all the possibilities and dividing by the number of people. But chances are that everyone in her class is normal, no matter how different they may seem. Bev, age thirteen, says, "Nobody feels as ugly as I do." She's wrong. You all know how much company she has!

If you feel in a state of turmoil, that's just how you should feel. You are! Everything is changing as your body changes. Your relationship with your parents, your teachers, and with each other—none of these can be the same as when you were a child. You are in transition to adulthood and that is just as wild and exhausting and wonderful and terrible as you are feeling. If you don't feel shook up now, then you just don't know what's going on.

The most difficult part of this period of tremendous growth and change is the fact that neither you nor anybody else can tell what you will be doing when you are finally grown up, whether or when you will marry, whether or when you will have children, what kind of work you will be doing, or where you will be living. No one at any age has any certainty about his future, but there are more open possibilities during the years of adolescence than at any other time. Peggy, age fourteen, described this feeling very well, when she wrote, "I feel a chill in this class. Maybe it's because I don't feel part of the class. I feel lost, running wild to some unknown place that I've never seen before." Or as Bill, age sixteen, commented, "If there's anything that scares me the most it would be the future. How am I going to earn money? When will I get married? Is my job good or bad? Will my wife be good or bad? Those things really bother me."

Another common and natural kind of feeling during this time of growth is a desperate wish to be free of parental controls one minute, and the next, feeling very afraid and wishing your parents would let you be dependent on them again. Harry, age sixteen, writes, "When my father tells me what time I have to get home, I want to punch him, and when I ask him a question and he says I have to make up my own mind, I get just as mad!"

It is time to try your own wings, to begin to take responsibility for your own life. Knowing that this is the direction you must move in, you begin to feel angry and rebellious at all parental rules and controls. But you also know that you are not yet ready to be an adult in full control of your own life, and that brings the scary feelings that make you wish you were about eight years old again. The trouble is that while you know you'll never be really grown up until you can move away from your parents, you also know that neither you nor your friends are ready yet to manage on your own.

At the very time when it feels right to start thinking for yourself and not listening to your parents so much, you also feel the way Shirley, age fifteen, feels: "I have been thinking and have decided that I am very much afraid of almost everything. It hurts to think that way, but I realize how much I shy away from things and try to make it look like I have all the confidence about something."

It may have occurred to you by now that you might have made almost any of the statements by young people I have already included. That may have shocked you, because another common characteristic of being twelve to sixteen is thinking that you are all alone and that your feelings are unique. You are unique, all right, and hopefully you will become more and more of a special individual as you grow, but the conspiracy among young people to hide their true feelings from each other is truly fantastic. There has never been an adolescent who hasn't felt scared, shy, self-conscious, unpopular, stupid, miserable. And that includes the ones you think are on top of the heap, having a ball. The cheerleader, the football captain, the smartest girl in your math class, and the most handsome boy in Sophomore English are as often the authors of the statements I've used or will be using as anyone else in your school.

The normal changes of growing are hard enough to deal with, but today's young people have more to contend with than most earlier generations. Change is so rapid now that even grownups aren't sure what's going on, what to believe in, what's right or wrong. There are many more opportunities and choices than there were before and that's both good and bad. It was easier in the days when boys knew exactly what kinds of work they could do and girls knew they would get married and be housewives and mothers. Now both men and women can do just about anything they want. It's a whole lot better in the long run, but it adds to the uncertainties and anxieties during these years of growing.

Jerry, age thirteen, said, "It makes everybody very uptight to live in such times. People hating each other, worrying about atomic bombs and if we've got enough oil for future generations, and whether we are going to be standing-room-only in the year 2000." Sara, age sixteen, wrote, "I didn't have as hard a time as many in my early years of maturizing. I have an older sister and she helped a lot and my parents are quite understanding. But what is hard on me is the neighborhood I live in, where nobody trusts each other and there's a lot of crimes, and I can't go out alone or at night. Why does everybody seem to hate everybody else?"

Bob, age thirteen, writes, "I live in New York City. My school looks like it might fall down any time. I can't stand the noise and the dirt. There are too many people all crowded together and that makes them unfriendly and really mean to each other. Sometimes, I hide my head in my hands and make up pictures in my head of some quiet, pretty place where I could just lie down and look at the sky."

While adolescence has always been a time of great physiological change, the emotional upheaval seems to become greater as the society in which young people live becomes more unstable and uncertain and as parents themselves become less sure of just exactly what they must teach their children and how they must discipline them.

Having said that adolescence is a very difficult stage to live through, does it necessarily follow that there is nothing you can do about it? Do you just have to suffer through it? Not at all. There are many things you can do about it, and beginning to understand your feelings is especially important. It is also important to remember that the pain and worry and fear and confusion of adolescence are not necessarily all bad. They can be a very important part of growing and learning.

What is *not* necessary is to feel alone and isolated. When you feel young and uncertain you lie to each other a lot. Something very interesting happened to the teachers who helped me collect comments from young people. One teacher wrote me: "At first I thought I would try to get reactions in class discussion. Almost nothing happened. Even though I knew that my students had all the normal problems of growing up, they were very uneasy about sharing their feelings with each other, openly. Most of them said everything was just fine. Then I asked them to write anonymously about how they *really* felt. I assured them that their compositions would be sent directly to you and would never be discussed in the classroom. You can see what happened; they all poured out their aching hearts!"

Each of you will feel better about yourself as you discover that your feelings are shared by your friends. You are not alone. I have a friend whom I've known since we were in grade school together. When our own children were teen-agers we began to reminisce about when we were young. I had thought of myself as fat, ugly, and unpopular; I was terribly jealous of Anne because I thought she was beautiful and all the boys were crazy about her. She was also rich and she went to a very fancy dancing class where there were some very handsome and popular boys that I had a secret crush on. When we were talking about our children, I said, "Oh, Anne, what do *you* know about teen-age suffering? You were beautiful and popular; you had a wonderful time!" She looked at me as if I was crazy. "Eda, I was *miserable*," she told me. "I thought I was horrible looking; I couldn't stand my face. I was scared to death of those boys in dancing school and I hated going. I was putting on a big act of being sophisticated and charming but inside I was shaking like a leaf. I envied *you* because you were editor of the literary magazine and got elected to the student council. *You* were the popular one!" Even though I was about forty years old when Anne told me this, I felt very relieved!

Understanding yourself is also the beginning of understanding others. As you come to understand some of the things that are happening to you, you can gradually begin to take responsibility for your own life and your future. You will have more compassion for other people, and deeper friendships will become possible. When you begin to accept and acknowledge the things that trouble you, you are well on the road to finding new satisfactions and joys in living.

2
Growing Up in a Family

You are probably thinking, "The last thing I want to read about is me and my family; that's the worst subject in the world—let's get to the interesting stuff!" The problem is that all the other things that you are thinking about and that are happening to you really do begin with the dramatic changes that are now occurring between you and your parents. And there are usually lots of problems because getting out of the nest and flying away is a lot easier on birds than it is on people.

Suzanne, age fifteen, writes, "For the past few years I have had the feeling that my parents and I were so different and had so little in common, that there was no way we could ever understand each other. I thought that this was due to the fact that I was an adopted child. But much to my surprise, when I told this to some of my close friends, they just laughed at me. They said they felt exactly the same way about their parents."

This feeling of being a stranger in one's own home is a very common and normal feeling during adolescence. Being a young child in a home is very different from being a person who is moving toward adulthood. Everything looks different; parents seem like invaders from another planet. You wonder—could these strange, unfeeling monsters *really* be the same people who once comforted you when you had a nightmare or were sick? Impossible!

Gail, age thirteen, says, "Why can't my mother understand girlish wishes? She hollers and yells and punishes me all the time. I know she must hate me. What is there between us that makes it this way?"

Ronnie, age twelve, says: "My family is forever visiting relatives and I am supposed to tag along. It makes me furious and we are always quarreling about this. Why can't my parents let me stay home or be with my friends?"

Barbara, age fourteen, says: "Why is it that you can do something with your friends and it will be great, and if you do the same thing with your parents —like a picnic or a party—it's awful?"

A great many of you feel that your parents are insensitive, unreasonable, inconsistent—a real pain, to put it bluntly. You are probably having more fights with them in one week than you used to have in a year when you were younger. Why?

Growing from childhood to adulthood is complicated in human beings and it takes a number of years.

If you think your parents are difficult, they think you are too. Adolescence scares many parents. Suddenly the nicest little kids seem to become raving maniacs. You shout and giggle and cry and talk on the phone for three hours to a friend you have seen all day; you want to wear all kinds of clothes and hair styles that seem crazy to them; one minute you are serious and steady, the next you are childish and irresponsible. They never know from one minute to the next what you are going to think or do. Right before their very eyes that pudgy little girl or boy has turned into a mixed-up stranger they don't know at all. And while they begin to wonder if it is really possible that you were ever that cute baby they once diapered and cuddled and carried around, you are climbing the walls trying to get out of that nursery image they have of you. If there is one thing you really can't stand right now, it's being reminded that you were also a baby and a young child—and the people who remember that time best are your parents.

How can this conflict ever be resolved? It may seem impossible to you right now, but every generation in history has managed to grow up and leave home, so you will too. But it's not easy.

In order to move away from childhood it is necessary to begin to separate yourself from your parents, and you do this by looking at them more critically. It helps to make that great plunge out of the nest easier if parents do not seem too wonderful. Your new feelings and observations also make you conscious of ways in which you are becoming very different from your parents; you are beginning to have ideas and opinions that have come out of your own experience, and these are often very different from those of your parents.

While young people can sometimes acknowledge their own feelings of strangeness, it can be very frightening when a parent agrees. Larry, age fifteen, tells of the time when he and his father were arguing about whether or not it was right for him to use swear words in front of his mother. Larry said his mother knew all the words—what was so terrible? His father, having grown up in a different time and a different world, thought that Larry should never speak this way before ladies. Larry muttered, "How could I possibly be a member of this Neanderthal family!" His father, in a voice trembling with rage, shouted, "You're right, you don't fit in this family any more." Larry said that for a moment he felt very frightened. It was painful to realize that both he and his father could feel like such strangers to each other. Once, when he was much younger, they had really been close. He added, "Later I apologized for being disrespectful and my father apologized for losing his temper, and I knew we still loved each other—but I also knew that once I became a man there would be a lot of ideas that would separate us from each other."

Another problem between parents and teen-agers is that you often have different priorities. Rebecca, age fourteen, writes, "All my mother worries about is being clean, keeping the house in order, and my getting good grades. What I have on my mind is being popular and pretty." David, fifteen, says, "All my parents worry about is what the neighbors will think. What I care about is what my friends will think."

Attitudes and ideas may also be very different. Alice, sixteen, says, "My parents act as if anybody with long hair is a drug addict." And Sam, fifteen, writes, "How can you be expected to get along with parents who think it's some kind of terrible sin if a girl and boy of different races or religions want to date each other? That's a prehistoric attitude and my generation just doesn't feel that way."

One thing that is important to remember is that not all new ideas are good and not all old ideas are necessarily bad. Rejecting all of your parents' ideas just because they come from an older generation is just as silly as accepting all the ideas of your friends just because they are more in tune with how things are now. Wisdom is not that easy to identify. As you go on growing and changing, you will be developing your own powers of critical judgment about what feels right and what feels wrong; what makes sense and what doesn't make sense; what is useful or helpful to you as an individual and what is not. In order to make your own best judgments, it is a good idea to do some hard thinking instead of just assuming that your parents know nothing and your friends everything.

Even when there are no specific differences in attitudes, the large majority of young people feel that their parents do not understand them. Margie, age sixteen, reports bitterly, "My parents are interested in exactly two things: high marks and I shouldn't get pregnant." Ken, age twelve, asks, "Why is it that parents never understand the things you *really* worry about?" Donald, age thirteen, says, "The problem at my house is the fact that we get yelled at for growing up." And Christine, age fourteen, says, "My father hollers if we forget anything we're supposed to do, as if we weren't supposed to ever forget anything."

Besides the fact that you are looking at your parents more critically than you ever have before and are likely to see them as real human beings, with human flaws, there are some other reasons why it seems they don't understand you at all. One reason is that they do remember a great deal about how they felt when they were your age—and that scares them. They know that growing up is a serious business; they remember some of their impulsive mistakes and they remember their own wishes, longings, and confusion. If adolescence is a tough time for you to live through, it was very much the same way for your parents, difficult as it may be for you to believe that they too were once young and vulnerable. Sometimes parents overreact to their own memories. They feel so frightened about your going through the same things they went through that they turn off their inner thoughts and memories. They don't understand you because they don't *want* to understand. Typical of this was the mother of a fourteen-year-old girl who told me, "I look at Audrey and I remember myself at her age. I remember the first and overpowering wish to be loved by a boy, I remember the fears, the crazy moods—and I begin to worry. I remember how my mother nagged and yelled and how I swore I would be a different kind of mother—but I'm not; I yell and nag too, and I hate myself for it."

Pam, age fourteen, wrote, "Parents think their kids will do the 'wrong' things they did when they were young." To some degree they are also envious; you are a constant reminder of their own years of youthful vitality. But mostly, it is their fears for your safety that make them behave in ways that make you confused and angry. They seem so arbitrary; some of the rules they lay down just don't seem to make any sense at all. They insist on a curfew and if you are a half-hour late they are ready to call the police. They will spend a fortune buying you school outfits you hate, but won't give you a big enough allowance to buy the jeans and shirts you really need. One week they are strict and punitive, the next they suddenly become very relaxed and don't seem to care what you do.

Some of the complaints about the unpredictability and unreasonableness of parents were expressed in these letters:

"I am twelve but I am treated like a baby at times. Yet other times I am fussed at for not acting my age."

"I am fifteen. My mother was *married* when she was seventeen. She says I can't go out on dates until I am sixteen!"

Kathy, age thirteen, writes, "My friends don't ask me to go some place with them. They say, 'Your father will come after you in two hours.' That's true. He just can't believe that I am old enough to know right from wrong."

Shirley, age fourteen, says, "Sometimes I wish my mother would care enough about me to keep me from doing certain things. She always says, 'Use your own judgment.' She should realize that sometimes I need to know what she thinks. That's what a mother is for, isn't it?"

You and your parents are both struggling to find some kind of balance between freedom and parental discipline. You feel very rebellious; you know that now you must learn more from your own direct experience and you feel ready for that challenge—most of the time. Fred, age sixteen, writes: "How can I show my parents I can make my own decisions? I'm not some dumb clown. What's going to happen when I'm eighteen—will I suddenly be struck with wisdom and be able to take care of myself? How will I learn to do that if they don't let me try?" Or, in a similar vein, Judy, age thirteen, says, "My parents complain I don't show any responsibility—but they won't give me any."

The problem is that while all of this is true, there are times when young people still do need some guidance; there are some mistakes that are best avoided if possible. Parents find themselves wondering all the time just how much to let go, how much to still try to keep in control. What usually happens is that in the daily arguments and battles, each side learns a little about the other, each gives a little, and as time passes, both parents and children begin to adjust to a new kind of relationship. But it is never easy for anyone.

Young people *can* be very irresponsible. You have so many things on your mind that you do forget to do some of the things you said you would. That makes a parent think to himself, "I guess George isn't ready to be treated any differently than when he was little." Sometimes the battle of wills reaches ridiculous proportions. A mother once told me that when her son was going out on a date she said to him, "Have a good time, Steve." He gruffly replied, "Don't tell me what to do!"

Freedom and independence are often tied up with the question of money. As you reach maturity, having money for your own use becomes more and more important. Elizabeth, age fourteen, says, "I try to proposition my mother into paying me for doing jobs around the house. She says, 'No.' How can I earn money? She says it's my duty to help. I agree, but I need to have some money of my own, and going to school, what kind of job can I get?"

Sometimes parents are afraid to let you earn money because they worry about what you will do with it. This is especially true since there has been so much real concern about the use of drugs. However, many teen-agers are able to explain what they need the money for and this reassures their parents. Mowing lawns, baby-sitting, doing painting and repair work on houses or apartments, taking care of plants and animals when people are away, walking dogs, making deliveries, and tutoring are some of the more common jobs that seem to be available.

Parents often feel that young people should participate as helpers in the home without being paid, simply as members of a cooperating group. What many families have done is to think together about certain jobs that are "extra"—not the ordinary kind of thing that has to be done every day. A parent will decide that a certain job is something they might have to allow an outsider to do, and so they pay a son or daughter for that special job. It might be cleaning out the garage, putting in a patio or retiling a bathroom floor.

One of the things that seems to anger teen-agers is when money is used as a means of discipline. Pat, age twelve, wrote, "I went to a skating rink one time when my father said I couldn't go. He stopped my allowance. I don't think my allowance had anything to do with skating." Pat is right. An allowance is most helpful in learning how to use money wisely and it gives teen-agers some feeling of independence when both parents and children view it as a fair share of the family's resources, given without strings. It should not be subject to discipline if it is going to help you learn how to use money. If you are serious and show that you are giving the matter a great deal of thought, you may be able to help your parents understand this point of view. A reasonable parallel to suggest might be to say that suppose Dad's salary was subject to his always behaving perfectly and never making a mistake.

An experience that is shared by most of you at some time during these years is a feeling of shame about your parents. After years of begging them to come to school plays and PTA meetings, now you want them to stay home. Kim writes, "My mother embarrasses me a lot. She gets silly and talks too fast and seems idiotic to me. I am trying to find a cure for her actions, but it seems hopeless."

In most cases, your parents really haven't gotten any more funny looking or peculiar than they ever were. You are just much more self-conscious right now, and so anything that seems to draw attention to you makes you feel uneasy. Once you feel more sure of yourself, your father's funny laugh or your mother's out-of-style dresses won't seem important. Right now you are so concerned with how you look and how others react to you that you also worry about the impression your parents are making.

When my daughter was twelve years old, I was supposed to go to a party at school as a chaperone. She said if I went, she wouldn't go. I had promised the principal I'd come, and I didn't see how I could get out of it. Finally we compromised; I would come, but I would stay in the back of the gymnasium where no one could see me. Now I know that I was not a different person when she was six or sixteen, when she didn't seem to think I was somebody to be ashamed of. It was just because she was twelve and so shy and embarrassed.

One of the areas of greatest disagreement between parents and young people has to do with clothes and general appearance. Twelve-year-old Phyllis writes, "My mother takes me shopping with her but I might as well stay home. She never lets me choose my own clothes anyhow. I always get what *she* thinks is nice."

Customs about dress and manners have changed more in the last 25 years than in the previous 300 years. To some degree you are a lot luckier than your older brothers and sisters who really had to put up a battle to fight for the new styles. Ten years ago, a boy wearing jeans and long hair might be suspended from school until he put on a shirt and tie and cut his hair. Most school codes of dress have been rapidly disappearing; the whole way of life has become more informal, and now, general neatness is usually sufficient. Even more, parents themselves have taken over some of the hair and clothing styles that were considered completely outlandish a few years ago. But strangely enough—or perhaps it's not so strange at all—if parents and children fight less about clothes, you can be sure they will find something else to fight about.

Another subject high on the list of complaints is curfews. That topic came up more often than any other in complaints about parents. When parents seem really unreasonable, it usually means they are very worried. If you want them to be more reasonable and flexible, you will have to find ways to reassure them. Compromises *are* possible. Gretchen, age sixteen, told us, "I had to do two things to work out reasonable rules about dating. First I promised to call home by eleven if I was going to be late, and second, I had to learn to respect my parents' right to a decent amount of sleep, so I usually came home at a reasonable time. When I showed I understood their worries, they never said a word on the rare occasions when I didn't get home until two or three A.M." Sal, age fourteen, said, "It was a battle every weekend, until I finally agreed that our neighborhood was dangerous, that I might get mugged, and I wouldn't travel alone at night, but stick with a group of friends."

What it is important for you to remember about all these areas of arguments is that they are realistic only in part. To some extent they are excuses that parents and children find in order to struggle through the problem of increasing independence for the child. It's a necessary ritual to help the parent get more used to letting go and the child to learn to struggle for independence. One psychologist, Dr. Fritz Redl, called this process "emancipation acrobatics." The ironic part of it is that sometimes the fighting is the worst the more parents and children happen to really love each other. The reason for that is that they feel safe in expressing their feelings and know for sure that there is real caring underneath.

Jenny, age twelve, writes: "As you grow you get in more arguments with your parents because when you grow, you want to get out of the house more. Your parents want you home in the early hours, so you stay out because your friends stay out. Sometimes your parents can't face you growing up and they treat you like you are still young." Jan, who is fifteen, is furious because her parents have told her that she may not go out with a group of people she met at the bowling alley. The boys are all eighteen and nineteen, out of high school, and working. They invite her to go dancing with them, and it makes her good and mad when her parents say no, she's too young. In the back of Jan's mind, if she is honest enough to admit it to herself, are some doubts and misgivings. She knows that the boys drink beer, and she has heard stories about their driving recklessly. She wants to be free and grown up and popular with an older crowd, which will be admired by her friends, but the truth of the matter is that she's also scared. In such situations, it is actually very nice to be able to blame everything on your "mean parents." You would love to go, but what can you do? You are stuck with old-fashioned, strict parents. Your friends feel sorry for you, and you feel both sorry and glad. That is a very common and natural experience.

On the other hand, Jonathan, age fifteen, is furious at his parents because they have refused to let him go on a camping trip during the summer with three of his best friends. They planned to be away from home for about a week. They love to hike and it would be a great adventure to eat and sleep outdoors. He really is ready for this experience, and his parents' fears may be quite unreasonable. Parents cannot always judge how ready a child is for a new experience, and of course they are sometimes wrong in the decision they make.

It is in families where there are very extreme attitudes that young people get so frustrated they may even consider running away from home. These are families where the parents may be extremely punitive or are severe disciplinarians, or appear to be uninterested and uncaring; where they are so busy with their work and their social lives they really neglect their teen-agers.

But running away from home is rarely a good solution. Jean and Rachel, both fifteen, lived in a large city. They were both fed up with all the restrictions their parents insisted upon. They both had a great love of animals. Rachel heard of a dog-boarding place that needed two girls to sleep at the kennels. During the day they would go to school, but after school they would clean out the cages and walk the dogs. In the evening they would feed them. Then they would sleep in a room near the cages. They would each earn $45 a week, which sounded like a fortune to them. There was a small kitchen where they could cook their meals. They begged their parents to let them try it for two weeks and see how it worked out. Their parents had great misgivings about it, but both families decided that this might be an important learning experience for their daughters, so after carefully investigating, they said O.K. The girls were ecstatic; freedom at last! For a day or two it was very exciting to do their own shopping and cooking. They met interesting people, and at first it was fun to take care of the dogs. But in a very short time they discovered that after a full day at school, they were tired. They didn't feel like cooking or washing laundry, and the work at the kennels was really so exhausting that they couldn't get their homework done. They were tired all day. The dogs barked a lot at night and kept them awake. After one week, they had the good sense to realize that they were not at all ready to be on their own. It was wonderful to go back home, to clean rooms and good meals and time to talk on the phone with friends; it even felt good to be arguing with their parents again.

There are some situations that do become quite intolerable, and when that is the case, young people can find better alternatives than simply running away. Pete went to live with a widowed aunt during his last year of high school because his family was too upsetting. There were eight children living in three rooms with alcoholic parents who fought constantly and were rarely able to work or care for the children. When a young person genuinely feels that living at home is simply beyond endurance, there are people who can help her make constructive plans. A favorite teacher, parents of a friend, the school nurse, a recreation leader, or a school adviser can help her find the community resources she may need.

3
Family Problems

Even in the most normal circumstances, life at home may often seem very difficult. Usually this occurs because of problems in communication. If parents and children could talk about their feelings openly with each other, that would make quite a difference. But one of the things that happens during adolescence is that mothers and fathers as well as their teen-age children find it more and more difficult to communicate with each other. Paul says, "Parents don't quite know how hard it is to talk to them if they look you in the face and yell so hard you can hardly figure out what they are saying half the time. I love my parents, but sometimes they make me so mad I want to just be by myself, and to get the madness out of my mind I turn the radio on and think of all the things they've done for me in the past." Probably the first thing that occurs to you in this connection is that your parents don't talk to you, they lecture you. This is a pretty fair observation. But maybe if you understand why, it will help you to feel somewhat differently about it.

Time often seems to drag for you—it seems that everything that's going to happen that's important to you is off in some distant future. Your parents feel exactly the opposite. They can't believe that you are now approaching adulthood. They get frightened; they wonder whether they have taught you the things you need to know in order to make good choices and decisions. In a kind of last-minute frenzy they feel they must tell you everything that is important to them. What they often forget or don't understand is that you know very, very well how they feel and what they think. Their ideas and values have sunk in far better than they—or even you—realize. And so, when you ask a question or seem unhappy or confused, or do things that worry them, they don't have a conversation with you they go into long speeches.

It is also hard for you to have a real discussion with them because you don't want to listen to them. Just think about the difference between talking to your parents and talking to a teacher you really like or some of your younger aunts and uncles. It is easier to talk to these people, or even ask their advice, for one simple reason: they are less likely to make you feel as if you are still a little kid. Your parents, in other words, are the people you turned to for love and comfort when you were little; deep inside you have the feeling that if you turn to them now for advice, suggestions, or opinions, you will be a baby again.

Sometimes parents talk at you so much and so hard that all you want to be able to do is turn them off. This is a kind of one-sided communication which drowns you out. At the other extreme, it can be just as painful when parents give you "the silent treatment." Ronnie, age fourteen, says, "When they just stop talking to you completely, then you know they have decided you are completely hopeless." That's the way it feels, but usually the real reason some parents resort to silence is that they feel helpless and don't know what to do to help. Or sometimes they really are very, very angry at something you have said or done which hurt them very much, and silence is their way of trying not to say things that would make the whole situation worse.

It is certainly not easy for a teen-ager to try to change the communication between himself and a parent—but it can be done, very gradually. If you were to say, "I know you're worried about me," this can help a parent know that you are really growing up. As you get older and have more self-confidence, you may even be able to say, "As soon as I ask you a question, you start to lecture at me. Couldn't we have a two-way discussion?" Or you might say, "It's hard for me to discuss my feelings with you because somehow you make me feel like a baby again." There is nothing in the world that can make a young person feel more sure that he is really growing up than to discover that there are ways in which he and his parents can move toward better understanding.

Some families have worked out what seems to be

quite a successful way of taking care of some of the natural grievances that arise; they hold family meetings once or twice a week where everybody can tell their gripes and try to work out some sort of compromises. Sometimes parents are not being mean but are just thoughtless. Claire, age fifteen, reports, "My parents were really taking advantage of me as a baby-sitter. I cried about it a lot. Every time they wanted to go out, they just told me I had to stay home and that was it. I talked to the guidance counselor in school about it and she said I should tell them the truth; that I didn't think it was fair, and that I never had a chance to have fun with my own friends. Much to my surprise, my parents really listened to me. I said I would baby-sit sometimes, but not all the time. We did work out a schedule."

Frequently the very last thing you want to have with your parents is communication. You just wish they'd leave you alone. Bob, sixteen, writes, "I have friends all over and I get a lot of mail which is delivered when I am at school. When I get home, Mother has always opened my letters. Not that I have anything special to hide, but it's the principle; it makes me very angry not to have any privacy." Leslie, age thirteen, wrote, "One day my parents were waiting for me when I came home from school. My mother was holding my personal diary. She had *read* it! I was so mad I could have killed her. She gave me all this stuff about parents having to know what's going on so they can protect their children. Of course they were very shocked by some of the things I wrote, but it was none of their business. I could never really trust them again." The feeling that one has no privacy is terrible. You need to have your own thoughts and fantasies without feeling that you are always being watched. It is also very annoying to many young people to have parents asking them questions after every date. "It's like being brainwashed," Kevin, age thirteen, says.

The reason given by Leslie's mother, that parents want to protect their children, is natural, if not always wise. A father told me that he was very much afraid his son was selling marijuana at his high school. He seemed to have a lot of new friends, spent much less time at home, and was spending money. He said, "I don't want to listen in on Steve's phone calls, I don't want to follow him around; but maybe, if I just try to pretend nothing is happening, my son will end up in prison!"

It is hard for many parents to realize that trust and respect are far more important in trying to save a child from disaster than snooping. When a young person feels that his parents really believe in his worth and judgment, they are much more likely to ask for help when they need it. It is possible that you can even explain this to your parents. Something like, "If you really want me to respect you, then I need to feel respected too." Or, "There are a lot of things I might *think* about or *write* about that have nothing to do with what I would really *do*. I need to feel my room and my possessions really belong to me. If I can't have confidence in that, then I will probably

32

become a sneaky person. Show me you trust me, and that will make me more honest with you."

A teacher asked her class to write compositions about privacy. There was not one single student in her class who felt that he or she had as much privacy as they needed. Some of the compositions were about fantasies of having a place where you could really be alone. These were "dream houses"—one had an underground railroad, in another you needed a special IBM card to be allowed in, and a third had rubber walls! Most teen-agers can well understand those wishes.

There are two things that can help. One is to understand that most parents snoop out of love and concern; it may be wrong, but that is still why they do it. The other thing to remember is that you can find ways to reassure your parents enough so that they will give you more privacy. Let them know that *you* know the things they worry about. And most of all you can reassure them by telling them that you are not just a sucker, listening to whatever anyone tells you to do, but that you are trying to think for yourself.

Privacy is a two-way street. Sometimes a good way to have people respect your privacy is to show you respect theirs. Mothers and fathers want privacy too. When was the last time you took your mother's best evening bag or your father's new belt without asking? Do you rush into their room without knocking? Do you feel free to look through your mother's desk or your father's dresser?

Another part of family life is living with brothers and sisters. It is sometimes a help if you have older brothers or sisters who can fight some of the battles for you ahead of time. Ben, age fourteen, says, "I have an older brother; he's three years older than me. He had a big fight about not cutting his hair and about learning to drive and staying out late—all sorts of things. Now, as I get older, my parents have a lot of the fight taken out of them!" Or Fran, age sixteen, tells us, "My parents are very shy and old-fashioned. They can't talk to me about boys and sex and things like that. But my sister is four years older and I can talk to her about anything."

The kinds of things that bug teen-agers about brothers and sisters usually have to do with jealousy and competition. Dan, age fifteen, says that his two older sisters are wonderful students, and all he ever hears is, "Why can't you study the way they do? Why are you such a bum?" It is natural to hate always being compared to someone else; you want to be yourself, not a carbon copy of anyone else. Larry, age thirteen, reports, "When I get mad at my brother it's because he always agrees with my father and I know why he does it, so he can get new shoes and clothes, sort of like kissing up to him or buttering him up."

Most children feel at one time or another that parents are showing favoritism to another child in the family. Penny, age fifteen, writes, "I have a brother, ten, and my mother pets him around, always buying him things, never me. I only get something for Christmas; for him every day is Christmas." Or Dennis, age

fourteen, says, "My older brother gets all the attention. Anything he does is O.K. But whatever I do is
wrong." Almost everybody who ever had a brother or
sister feels that parents are often unfair. Jim, age
fourteen, says, "My brother and I have jobs to do
around the house but somehow I nearly always wind
up doing his job too. This does not seem fair to me
because I get blamed if his jobs aren't done." Or Mar-
ian, age thirteen, says, "I have an eight-and-one-half-
year-old sister. I could kill her. She walks in and does
whatever she wants with my belongings, but if I ever
touch her things, she goes screaming to Mom and
gets petted. I'm supposed to be some kind of angel
because I'm older." Deloris, age sixteen, says, "My
brother and I have to do all the work because our
sister is treated like a baby even though she's nine
years old." Sometimes jealousy and feelings of unfair-
ness work in reverse. Judy says, "My older sister is
very jealous of me because I'm prettier and more
popular. She calls me all kinds of bad names and we
fight a lot."

Many young people feel that they are being over-
burdened with the care of younger children at a time
in their lives when they need to be with their own
friends. Marcia, age fourteen, writes, "My mother ex-
pects me to take my ten-year-old sister along when I
go out with my friends. She has no idea how terrible I
feel." Or on the opposite side, Sheila, age fifteen,
complains, "My older brothers tease me all the time
and my parents think it's funny."

Sometimes problems with brothers and sisters occur

because parents seem to expect you to behave the same way as other children in your family. Joan writes, "I have an older sister who got pregnant when she was fifteen. I also have a younger brother who plays hookey a lot. Me—I'm not perfect, but I like school and I don't think I'm like my sister. But my parents act to me like I'm going to get into trouble all the time, just because the other kids are giving them a hard time. It's not fair to be treated like I'm going to turn out bad."

No one can tell you that there is a simple solution for any of these problems; they are a natural part of family life. But you can make them somewhat more tolerable, if you understand why you feel the way you do.

All children want their parents to see them clearly and separately as unique human beings. Rivalry is almost inevitable since it is hard for parents to do that all or even most of the time. It is also true that just because you and your brothers and sisters are so different, your parents react differently to each of you. It is easier to get along with a quiet, easygoing child than with a rambunctious one; parents get madder at the lively one usually. That doesn't mean they don't love both children. Some children are harder to raise than others—they were just born that way. Sometimes a child will remind a father of a brother who was always getting away with murder when he was a child, and he acts toward his son more as if he were that brother than a child of his own. Or a mother sees the same qualities in one daughter that she sees in herself, and if she doesn't like certain

36

things about herself, she gets angrier at that child than another child who is not as much like her.

When you feel that your parents are being unfair or unjust, their attitudes sometimes have little to do with you, directly. And equality and fairness are the last thing anybody really ever wants!

Sometimes when you shout at a parent, "You're not fair!" you are really asking for something you don't want at all. You are really saying, "I want to be treated *the same*." Parents get confused; they wonder, "Do I really love one child more than the other? Am I unfair?" Then they may try to treat you and your brothers and sisters exactly the same way, but instead of liking that, you may find yourselves just getting angrier and more upset. The reason is that nobody ever wants to be treated the same as anybody else. That would mean that we were all exactly alike, and we are not. The fact that we are all different is really the very best part of us. You and your brothers and sisters are different ages, you have totally different personalities, different interests, different talents, different weaknesses. What you really want most is to be seen as a separate and special person. Explain this to your parents.

The problems of getting along with brothers and sisters sometime seem absolutely horrendous. But they are the normal problems of people of different ages and temperaments who are trying to live together. One psychiatrist dismissed "sibling rivalry" by saying to a group of parents, "So long as the children avoid bloodshed, you're ahead of the game!"

But not all family problems are so normal. Many young people have very special problems in family living. Parents are separated or divorced, one parent may be an alcoholic or drug addict. A parent may be mentally ill or a chronic invalid. These days lots of parents are unemployed. In many families mothers and fathers fight a lot with each other. Sometimes a parent has died. Sometimes a parent may be in prison. Under any such circumstances, teen-agers suffer a great deal. These are heavy burdens especially when they are added to the natural ups and downs of being an adolescent.

When there are special problems of this kind, almost invariably children tend to blame themselves in one way or another for what is happening. You think to yourself, "If we had been better kids, Dad wouldn't have deserted the family," or, "If I wasn't such a poor student and if Mom hadn't worried about it so much, she wouldn't be in the mental hospital now." Parents have many problems, which come from their own earlier life experiences, long before you were born. Their children are *never* to blame in any way. A parent would not stop drinking, or hitting other people, no matter how perfectly you were to behave.

Another important thing to remember is that feeling angry is perfectly natural and nothing to feel guilty about. You feel ashamed in front of your friends—you don't want them to know your parent is crippled or in trouble with the law or has violent outbursts of temper. It makes you feel angry—you wish you could have different parents, or that the parent you are ashamed of or who makes your life so hard would go away and never come back. That is a natural feeling and it won't hurt anybody. Feelings only get in the way when they lead to unsuitable actions. Sandy, age fifteen, often felt great resentment toward his father, who had deserted the family; but his resentment didn't keep him from working after school every day at the supermarket to help with the family finances. Heather, age fourteen, felt frightened and shy about her mother being in a mental hospital, but that didn't stop her from visiting her and bringing her some flowers. We can't help the kinds of feelings we have, and we shouldn't try to stop them, because that often makes them worse; what we do have control over is what we do about the feelings.

Just because parents have problems, that does not mean that you will necessarily have the same problems. Mental illness, alcoholism, or violent temper are not inherited characteristics. Today we know much more about these problems than we ever did before and people can get help. You can learn more about the special problem there may be in your family by reading or by talking to adults who can help you understand. When such things really trouble you, your doctor or school guidance counselor can help you find someone to talk to who is a specialist in understanding emotional problems. The more you understand your own reactions and some of the reasons for your parents' troubles, the more you will be able to have a very different kind of life yourself.

One of the most common special problems in a

family is a stepparent. Jeanne, age fifteen, describes the most usual problem as "we just don't merge." Jeff, age twelve, writes, "My father is married again, to a woman who is twenty-eight years old. I've tried to like her but she never talks to me. They've been married a year and I am thinking of running away." Nina, fifteen, says, "My mother got married after my father died and my stepfather's a nice man but there is some kind of barrier between us. I think he wishes my mother didn't have me to worry about."

Divorce has become so common in recent years that chances are you know many young people with stepparents, if you don't have one yourself. People are beginning to understand the complicated problems involved much better than they used to, and many families are able to talk quite openly about the way they feel. It is hard for a new parent to walk into a home and take over; it is equally hard for a child to adjust to a new parent. There are likely to be hidden resentments, self-consciousness, uneasiness on both sides. It takes time and effort on everyone's part to make a successful adjustment. It is natural for you to feel resentful, uneasy, and oversensitive. At the same time, it is possible to recognize that time and patience and a willingness to compromise are necessary to a solution, and you must believe that your life need not be ruined by these problems.

In conclusion, when you think about your family it often helps to try to keep things in perspective and remember that some of the things that annoy you the most are really the most important things in your lives. People usually get angry at each other when they care about each other a lot.

Jack, age sixteen, wrote, "A lot of my friends are always complaining; their parents say, 'Do this' or 'Do that.' My father left me and my mother, and she has to work every day for long hours. I spend a lot of my time alone. Sometimes I wish I had parents yelling at me to do something."

Brenda, age fourteen, writes, "I don't know who my father was. My mother told me she had her marriage annulled before I was born. Now that I'm older, I wonder if she was ever married at all—not that it makes much difference to me. She didn't want me either and I live with my grandparents, who are good to me. But sometimes I get terribly depressed and just want to cry and cry. I have my own room and plenty to eat but I feel like a lost child." That is the other side of living with parents who may drive you crazy, but who still make you feel loved. As Josh, age fifteen, said after a big fight with his family, "I guess you really wouldn't know you were growing up if you didn't have your parents to put down!"

What you are feeling most strongly about your parents during these years is ambivalence, which means you have at least two different kinds of feelings about them at the same time; you love them and you hate them. You love them because they were the people who took care of you when you were little and you hate them because they are a constant reminder of that earlier time, and that seems to make it harder for you to deal with the task before you which is to become an independent adult.

It takes a great deal of courage to grow up. It would be safer and quieter and a lot less trouble to go on acting like a baby, letting parents decide everything and telling you what to do. Then there would be no fights, no anger—and no guilty feelings for things said or done in anger. Then there would be no important decisions to struggle with, no mistakes to learn from. You'd just never grow up. There are a few young people in every generation who do just that; they are so afraid of making their parents angry at them, they are so timid about facing life, that they remain very passive and obedient. Such people never do become independent adults leading their own lives.

It takes even more courage to rebel when you have had a pretty good and comfortable life at home. But fortunately, there is a deep instinct inside you that pushes you toward the adventures of your own growing up. You just can't sit still; you have to go on struggling to be a mature person, and so you continue to fight your parents' authority. More and more parents are beginning to understand that this is a good and healthy sign, and painful as the process may be, the end result will be a strong, free, sensible, wise young person. You will be amazed at how proud they will become as you reach maturity.

4
School–Who Needs It?

It might be logical to assume that since it is difficult to spend a great deal of time with one's parents during the years of adolescence, going to school would be a happy solution to the problem. That is a logical theory if one were to avoid asking teen-agers themselves how they feel.

"It's true your teachers treat you a little more dignified than your parents," said Grace, age thirteen. "But your parents really follow you into the school, with their worries about how you are doing."

Julie, also thirteen, wrote: "One of my main problems in junior high school is my grades. I always worry about being as near perfect as my mother expected me to be. Report card time came around and I hadn't done well. I was so scared of what my mother would say that I decided not to show her my report

43

card. My mother always told me I could talk to her about anything. When I finally showed her the report card she started screaming and yelling about how dumb I was. You can imagine how this made me feel. What can a child do to protect her ego?"

The large majority of students I talked with or who wrote to me seemed very preoccupied with failure and are constantly worrying about tests and about passing from one grade to the next. Lewis, age fifteen, wrote, "It is very hard to really learn anything when all you can think about is passing or failing. I am a very curious person and I am very interested in American History, for example. But it seems I spend most of my time memorizing facts, like the dates of wars. Tests make you lose interest in interesting subjects." Susan wrote, "I am what you might call a 'Nature Girl.' I have a lot of pets and I also love flowers and things like that. The one thing I really looked forward to in high school was studying Botany and Biology. The first week in class we had to begin to memorize all that stuff about classification, like 'kingdom, phylum, class, order, family, genus and species.' On the first test I got a C minus. I was so turned off, it nearly broke my heart." Allen, age sixteen, wrote, "In school I feel like a machine, some kind of robot that's supposed to memorize a lot of stuff and then repeat it on a test. Of course, then you forget that information while you memorize the next things."

It is easy to understand that when one feels a great sense of pressure about tests and grades, they become associated with fear and anxiety and not with learning. It is important to remember that if we are interested in knowing more about a subject, we *do* have to study, memorize, and practice new skills. It helps to keep in mind that the test is really *for you*, to help you measure your own progress. That is far more important than trying to compete with others or please parents or teachers.

In addition to strong negative feelings about tests and marks, the subject of most unhappiness was homework. Sheila, age fifteen, told me, "I start at six o'clock. I take a half-hour for supper. Maybe another half-hour to do something else for recreation, like talk to a friend on the phone or watch a TV program. Then I study until eleven P.M. That's every day. Six hours in school, then about four more hours at home. I guess the way that we all stand it is that everybody is suffering together, so it's not like you're all alone."

Barbara, age thirteen, said, "My parents don't understand that I just can't study unless I play the radio very loud. It *helps* me to concentrate. They keep turning it off." Holly, age fourteen, writes, "My parents go over my assignments every night. If they think I'm goofing off, they don't allow me to watch any television. They sit and watch it all night and tell me they have to relax from working all day. I'd like to know what they think I've been doing!"

Even though the numbers were few, there were some positive responses to questions about school. Amy, age fifteen, said, "At my school there is a whole new system about homework. There was a student-faculty committee that worked on this for five years.

45

Needless to say, we have a wonderful principal, but he really just gave us the chance—we had to do the work. In almost every class now, we get special assignments to do things we can't do in the classroom. Like go to a museum or the zoo or historic places or the college observatory or a hospital or some kind of social agency, and write something about what you find out. We are also allowed to do volunteer work as a substitute for homework in some classes. What I like best is for my Civics class I had to interview businessmen and politicians, people like that. We get discount prices to plays and concerts and if we write reports, that's also for homework credit."

Larry, age sixteen, told about a fascinating project: "In our high school we have an introductory course in psychology. The teacher let us choose our first project, which was to check out about homework and listening to the radio or some other type of distraction. We did experiments that proved scientifically that some people work better in silence and some work better with a lot of noise. We mimeographed the report and every student took it home to show his parents. That was really a great experience!"

Connie, also sixteen, reports that her high school now offers new subjects in preparation for a much wider selection of special interests and vocational planning. She says, "Now you can study nutrition, ballet, how to become a nurse's aide or a salesman. School is as interesting as real life!"

For those of you who have not been this fortunate, the first challenge is to acknowledge your angry or frightened or hopeless feelings about some aspects of school. The next step is not to feel helpless and victimized. Sometimes you can help to bring about necessary changes. Victor, sixteen, wrote, "We had a math teacher who was out of his skull. Even the best students in the class were failing his tests. His homework assignments could take two hours a night. We had a meeting and formed a committee to go talk to him. He was furious and said the problem was we were all spoiled and lazy. So we went to see the Dean of Students. About a week later we got a notice to meet with the teacher, the Dean and the Head of the Math Department. We were really scared. We were asked a lot of questions and the teacher had to show some of his tests and assignments. We figured we'd never get out of there alive; everybody was so serious and stern-looking. Next thing we know, the Head of the Math Department is agreeing with us! Right in front of us he says this would be O.K. if we were an advanced class and if no other teacher was giving homework, but it's too much pressure. Now, nobody ever got to like that teacher, but we did change things a lot."

Students and educators who have wanted to bring about changes have failed some of the time. But they have also succeeded. There have probably been more changes in junior and senior high schools in the last ten years than in the previous one hundred. Many of these changes are often quite spectacular. Some of you are now attending schools where you feel truly respected as a person and where you eagerly look forward to each day's learning. Such schools didn't just happen; they were the result of hard work on the part of teachers, parents, and students, who felt that change was necessary. Josh, age sixteen, attends an alternative school on Long Island in New York. He told me, "I wake up every morning so excited and happy, I can't believe it!" In Josh's school a student-faculty committee plans the full curriculum with each student taking responsibility for developing his own program. The school is made up of 105 students who chose not to continue the regular high school program. They meet in four rooms set aside in the high school building as well as in each other's homes. They have five regular faculty members assigned by the Board of Education, and the students and teachers are permitted to hire a certain number of people in the community to teach special subjects—a businessman for Economics, a nursery school teacher for Child Development, a retired lawyer for a course in Government. Josh commented, "Anybody who thinks this is a lazy way out of school work is wrong. We work harder than we ever did before. We *want* to."

Another experimental program that is being tried in many parts of the country is what is sometimes called "a school without walls." For example, in Philadelphia there is a high school that is set up in such a way that students do a great deal of study and research on their own, outside the school building, reporting back to advisers and meeting for discussions of their projects.

Some of you may have also heard about schools that are called "street academies." These are usually schools which meet in stores or other unused buildings and are supported by private foundations at least in part. They are designed for young people who are so turned off by traditional schools that they have left school or have gotten into so much trouble they have been expelled from school. The curriculum is planned for each student individually according to his needs and interests.

In most places the junior and senior high schools are too big. It would be better if there were never more than twenty or twenty-five in a class and if no grade level had more than 100 to 150 students in it. Because this is a time when you need the advice and reassurance of adults who are *not* your parents it would be a great help if each of you had more intense relationships with teachers instead of running from class to class all day. Instead of having eight teachers a day it might be better if you had two, three, or four, who taught all the subjects, and whom you could get to know more intimately.

Many educators feel that too many schools focus on subject matter exclusively, rather than on helping students learn to develop good human relationships. They feel that more attention must be paid to the training of teachers who love young people and are excited about learning.

A real problem in education at all levels is that as the population soared and schools got bigger and bigger, it seemed necessary to hire more and more people to run them. School administrators became increasingly powerful as they were brought in to keep things running smoothly. Considering the problems of time, space, and numbers of people and classes they deal with, they do a very good job, but it often seems to those of you who go to big schools that students and even teachers have become less important than the administration.

Tremendous and rapid increase in population also accounts at least in part for the great emphasis on tests and grades. But it is clear that less learning takes place the more anxious and tense a student feels. What we must work hard to solve is how to see to it that in spite of the numbers of students, our schools do not get so big that individual needs cannot be met. We need to set up testing programs and grading systems that measure individual growth instead of comparisons with other students.

Probably the single greatest problem for the schools —and therefore for you—is the rapid rate of change that effects the whole society. Dorothy, age fifteen, writes: "Most of my life at school has nothing to do with anything that's on my mind. It's got nothing to do with real life, either. Let me tell you about my school. There are 6,000 students. Everybody must take English, Math, and History. Most of the students are more interested in smoking grass and making out. A lot of the girls are pregnant and not married. There is a lot of venereal disease too. I learned a lot my first week in high school, but it wasn't in the classrooms."

Dorothy's feelings and attitudes are due in large part to an out-of-date system of education that just cannot keep pace with all the changes taking place in society. More students from more different kinds of backgrounds are caught in social upheaval, in such rapid advances in technology that nobody has time to decide how automated they really want their lives to become. Our educational system tends to reflect whatever is happening to society as a whole, and these are, indeed, shook-up and difficult times.

It is not the fault of the school system alone if school seems meaningless or frightening; schools can only change and develop into better instruments for learning when communities are willing to do something about them.

But what do you do about your feelings of anger and disappointment? You can turn off and cop out; you can say, "I'm not going to buck the system—I'm just going to get by." You can decide to "pay them back," by goofing off or making trouble. These "solutions" hurt you, and don't help anyone.

It makes much more sense to try to work for change where this is possible, and to accept your feelings of anger and disappointment. You will be learning perhaps the most important lesson you may ever learn, that nothing in life is ever perfectly wonderful or perfectly terrible, but a mixture of both, and that there are always ways of changing things, even if it is only inside your own head.

Even if you are going to a crumbling, leaky, creaking old school in a slum neighborhood, somewhere in that school building there are some teachers who really care what happens to you. You have to look for them and let them know you want and need their help. It is strange but true that whether you decide to go to a private prep school or a public school, by the time you graduate from high school, you will probably have had about five teachers whom you will remember for the rest of your life. And that can be enough. A truly inspired teacher can get you excited about learning, open up new areas of interest, and, most of all, make you feel so good about yourself that you find your own new ways of learning in and out of school.

"I hated school and was sure I was going to leave the minute I was sixteen," wrote Selma. "But when I was a junior I met an English teacher who changed my life. Now I'm seventeen and I'm going to finish high school. First of all she asked us to write about our feelings. I kept a daily diary which was private, between her and me. Secondly, she corrected my spelling and grammar but she marked me on my ideas and how well I communicated. And most of all, she treated me like I was *somebody important*. I still hate a lot of things in school, but now I know better what I want."

Wherever there is a library, there can be discovery in reading. Wherever there is a laboratory, a gym, a student council, teachers, and other students, there is something you can find on your own to make life more interesting. If there is some subject that interests you very much but is not offered, it is frequently possible to start an after-school club. One student told me that he was interested in transcendental meditation and read several books about it, but never mentioned it to anyone else, "because I was sure they'd think I was some kind of screwball." One night he went to a meeting about Yoga at a local YMCA and discovered three other boys from his school. They decided to organize a club, and within a year there were thirty-five students attending regularly who had raised enough money to have an expert come and meet with them and teach them some Yoga techniques for meditating. One school has a club dealing with American antiques; another high school group is studying extrasensory perception. Another school happens to have so many students interested in music and drama that they put on several Broadway musicals every year, on their own time.

Paula, age fifteen, wrote: "There was a rule in our school that boys took shop and printing and girls took cooking and sewing. Some of us decided this was ridiculous and old-fashioned and should be changed. A group of girls put a notice in the school paper asking to meet with any boys who would like to take cooking classes. About ten boys came to our meeting, and we formed a committee to go talk to the principal. It took a whole year before anything happened, but now anybody can take any of these subjects. What really helped us is that we went to give a speech about it to the PTA and they really backed us up. It was great. We never thought they'd agree with us, but almost all of them did."

What we must all work hard to do is to bring a broader variety of courses into the school curriculum so that high school does become more relevant to what is happening to you in the real world. Parents, students, and teachers have succeeded in many places in petitioning for new kinds of courses—preparation for marriage and parenthood, psychology, the history of music and art, sex education, family relations, weaving, modern dance—subjects that should be as respected and taken as seriously as any of the more traditional subjects.

No matter what difficulties or inadequacies there may be in any school, no one can ever stop anyone from thinking and feeling. You can change your life by what you do inside your head as much as what you can do on the outside. That is where your life and your future really are at: inside of you. The question is, do you care enough about yourself to find ways to enrich your own life, and can you sit down and think about what would help you to do this? If most of the subjects you are required to take bore you, you can take a few evening courses at a college or community center on your own. Or you can work as a volunteer in a field that interests you. This almost always improves one's school assignments, because feeling good makes everything go better.

One of the things you may need to work on is what you think about success and failure. Felice, age fourteen, wrote, "I have a very good biology teacher this year. He told us that penicillin was discovered by accident. We were really very surprised. He explained that in order to find out anything new, you really have to take chances, you have to take risks. Otherwise you never find out what might work or not. I began to think about what happens to us in school. We worry so much about failing, we don't want to try anything new."

Anger, nervousness, and tension usually have more to do with failing than anything else. It would be wonderful if there was less emphasis on grades; it would be even more wonderful if there wasn't constant reference to where you will be and what you will be doing five or ten years from now. As Lester, age fourteen, wrote, "I get the feeling that nothing I'm doing right now matters right now. I have to get good marks to go to college. That's four years from now. Why is it that children are forced to live only for the future?"

It would be nice if more schools were designed to allow each student to pursue his own special interests and talents. It would be nice if parents and teachers never made you feel scared of failing and ashamed of getting low marks. But until that happens, what you *can* change is how you *feel* about what you are doing. Randy, fifteen, said, "I made up my own mind that I needed to get through high school, and that I was not dumb, no matter what anybody said. I was not dumb, I just learned better from doing things than trying to learn them from books. I decided I was not going to get mad and I was not going to get scared. I get mostly C's and D's, but I am not quitting and I am not failing. I will get through—and then I will find the kind of work that will make me feel smart."

It will help you greatly if you will believe this truth—that failing in high school rarely reflects stupidity! Most commonly it means that you are too anxious about failure. Feeling angry because you are bored or hate the subject also causes failure on tests. Feeling that you are in school just to please your parents or your teachers can cause failure. If you can come to the conclusion that you'd rather not fail because that will *interfere with your own goals*, you will be halfway home. If you can try to learn what is interesting to you about each subject and if you can apply it to your own life, that will help with exams too. Even if you do fail sometimes, that is not the end of the world. Some people who do very poorly on tests succeed remarkably once they find the field of their greatest interest and ability. Sometimes people get poor marks on tests because they can think of thirty different reasons why three or four of the multiple-choice answers might be justified. They are always thinking about new possibilities. Such a person may do poorly on tests—but can turn out to be a bright and creative person later in life.

Failure often has to do with distraction, and there is no time in your life when you will be more distracted than you are right now. It is very hard to concentrate on the laws of geometry when you are dying of shame because your face is covered with acne, or you're trying to get up the nerve to ask a very popular girl to go to the football game, or when you left home this morning your parents were screaming at each other and threatening to get a divorce, or you want to try out for the basketball team but you're afraid you're too short and they'll laugh at you.

Emotional problems have much more to do with an inability to focus attention than poor teaching or irrelevant subjects. Feelings interfere with studying, memorizing, paying attention. Sometimes it is easy to figure out what's on your mind. Other times you have no idea what's making it impossible for you to remember anything. This is one of the major reasons why schools usually provide guidance and counseling services. More and more towns and cities also have mental health clinics and educational advisory services. It may be that you need help in finding out what unconscious thoughts and feelings are getting in the way of your being able to study. Each of you has probably met at least one or two people you really admire and can talk to, and asking for help is a sign of strength and courage. It shows you have self-respect and want the best in life for yourself.

There are a few students for whom high school does become intolerable. There are just too many other problems, too much restlessness, too many feelings of inadequacy and unworthiness and maybe just no opportunities to do the things one can do well. All is *not* lost if a student decides to drop out at sixteen. Sometimes working for a while—or finding out how hard it is to get a job—is a necessary part of growing up. Sometimes working at a job one really enjoys for a while gives one the self-confidence to want to go back and get that diploma. It is *not* true that it is harder to study later on, or that it is impossible or even more difficult to catch up. If you just feel you'll blow your brains out if you have to stay another day

—then it is time to get some help. Try to talk it over with someone you like and trust, someone who may be able to help you get a job or take some special courses or find an apprenticeship in some job that interests you. Leaving school should not be a disgrace or a disaster if you have a plan and some sense of purpose. And if it turns out to be a mistake, that's a good thing to have learned; the work will go a lot better when you come back.

Nancy wrote a composition called "High School Is a Waiting Game." Her point of view was that people just don't know what else to do with teen-agers, so they stick them in school. As a matter of fact, this isn't really such a terrible reason for schools. These can be years of real growing in a relatively safe place in which to try those wings. We live in such complicated times that a "waiting game" can be very important. You need time to grow, time for making smaller jumps out of the nest before the really big ones.

School is a place for testing oneself and gaining new strengths. It is a place for gaining self-confidence, slowly but surely as the years pass. You need time in which to accumulate some important information. You need skills that will help you survive without having to depend on others to take care of you later on. During the turbulent years of adolescence, one needs to be with other people who are going through the same experiences. You can comfort and reassure each other and you can also turn for advice and guidance to grownups who are not your own parents. It is a place where parents are certainly in less control than at home. As Hilda, age fourteen, put it, "One thing is for sure—if I had to stay home all the time, I'd really go crazy!" Another important value is that high school can offer you a smorgasbord; it offers a variety, a wide assortment of subjects and activities, and gives the student a chance to begin making some choices, testing his or her interests and natural aptitudes. It is a chance to have a few close relationships with those special and never-to-be-forgotten teachers who turn you on to learning and to yourself. It is a place for nonacademic experiences as well, from cheerleading to acting Shakespeare, from electioneering for student council members to playing in a jazz quartet.

But most of all, according to every student who told us anything about his or her experiences and feelings, "School is *the place where you are with people your own age*, and that's the most important part of it. Making friends." And that is a whole other subject.

Friends

If adolescence is the time during which you move from childhood to adulthood, what could be more fitting and logical than that your greatest concern should be with those you are going to spend that adulthood with.

In addition, as you begin to loosen the ties to your family, you are bound to feel scared and uncertain, and need some moral support. You may wonder why, if you and your friends think about each other so much and need each other so much, you can manage to get into so much trouble with each other.

There are very good reasons for this. When you are feeling uncertain and unsure of yourself, what you want most in all the world is to be reassured—and the only people who can give you that reassurance are just as mixed up as you are.

Few, if any, of you can talk about all your worries openly, but in written compositions and letters, these are the kinds of concerns that *all* young people have:

Carlos writes, "I am fifteen and very short. Many people think that height makes no difference, but I think it does. I don't mind so much being called 'Shorty' but the kids treat me different. They seem to pet and baby me. They don't know it hurts a lot." Tina, fourteen, writes, "I don't have many friends because I am the teacher's pet. People think you are too studious. I want to get a scholarship to college and I need to get good grades and have the teachers like me, but not if it makes me unpopular." Candi, fourteen, says, "When I feel down I feel like going to my friends and tell them what worries me. Sometimes I feel they don't want to help me and I am afraid to trust them. I feel like some of my friends might talk about me behind my back."

Some other comments, frequently repeated in other ways, were: "Popularity, even friendship, is based on looks. Teen-agers don't look for the good parts inside."

"How can I adjust to being an outcast?"

"Sometimes I'm afraid to give my ideas because if my ideas are rejected, I feel rejected too."

Popularity is the most common concern among young people from twelve to sixteen. Being well liked becomes more and more important when you realize that you will be leaving the safety of your family and will be judged by people your own age. It is a time of life when being different becomes almost more than you can bear. Sometimes these feelings become especially strong when you move from elementary school to junior high school and from there to senior high school. Just at a time when you don't want to shake things up you are forced to do so. A seventh grader wrote, "I was very frightened by thoughts of going to junior high. New experiences coming all at once is scary for a shy twelve-year-old. I missed the security of the small grammar school and all the friends I'd grown up with. So many people in one place, you tend to have your identity smeared. You are part of something so big instead of being a separate person."

This is a very big adjustment and it takes time. The more nervous and anxious you feel, the harder it is to begin to make new friends. Or even keep old ones, for that matter, since feeling insecure, shy, and embarrassed makes you so uptight it is almost impossible to make warm, genuine contact with someone else, which is what friendships are all about.

If you still think you are the only one who is worried about being popular, how do you account for the fact that almost nobody dares to be different, right now? There are always a few brave or indifferent people—or sometimes a young person feels so defeated, so lonely and frustrated, he may give up altogether—but on the whole, you and your schoolmates worry desperately about looking just right; one year that means long hair, another it means short; it may mean mini-skirts or it may mean patched jeans; in one year there may be a sweeping change from pants cuffs to no pants cuffs, from layers of heavy makeup to no makeup at all. The biggest fights that go on at home have to do with a parent's expectations that you will please wear last year's clothes because you have not outgrown them—when you would rather die than be caught in last year's styles.

You are *all* worrying about what others will think of you, you are *all* worrying about being laughed at, you are *all* worrying about what others say about you behind your back—and that is why it is frequently true that while you *all* want each other's friendship and love, there is often as much heartache as comfort. It is as if a whole family were to get the flu at one time, so that there was nobody strong enough to take care of anybody else.

What happens is that each of you, in your natural desire to be accepted and to achieve social success, tries to figure out just what is expected of you. You are prepared to pay a price for popularity. The problem is that the less you become your own unique and special self, the less likely it is that you will make genuine friendships.

Lynn writes, "I am fifteen years old and by nature, I suppose you might call me a tomboy. I lived on a ranch until I was nine and I love horses and ride well and like to be very active, physically. Now I go to a high school where probably none of the kids have ever seen a horse, much less a ranch! The girls are all trying to be sweet and cute, and I feel like a clown. For two years I have tried and tried to be like them, but it isn't working out. Sometimes I wonder if they might like me better if I stopped trying to be like them."

Marvin, age fourteen, said, "I have been playing the violin since I was six. I guess you might say I am very talented. Last year I won a scholarship for a year's free lessons with one of the best teachers in this city. I decided not to do it. At school the other kids were calling me silly pet names like 'the little old string plucker.' I decided to give up practicing for a while, until I feel better with kids my own age. If I want to be popular I will have to be good at some sport, I guess."

During the uncertain years of adolescence, some young people will sell their souls to be well liked— and in the long run, it never works out. That is the tragedy. We think the road to social acceptance lies in being what others want us to be; then we find out everybody feels the same way. The less each person is truly himself, the more difficult it becomes, in this artificial atmosphere, for anyone to feel truly friendly toward others or to attract genuine admiration for himself.

In addition to everyone trying to dress the same way and talk the same way and do the same things, there is another almost universal symptom of general insecurity, and that is the amount of lying and boasting and showing off that goes on among teen-agers. One teen-ager wrote, "Often everyone is talking about a topic you don't know anything about. You pretend so you're not left out. Maybe *nobody* knows what he's talking about!"

A teacher told me that one day, when she had stayed late in school to finish up some work, she met two of her students in the deserted parking lot. They were holding hands and looking at each other shyly. They were terribly embarrassed when the teacher appeared. She suggested it was time for both of them to get home, and that she would be glad to drop them off, since she passed their homes. When Phillip got out of the car, he kissed Pat on the cheek, and they both turned bright red and said good-by. Pat was overcome with shyness and said nothing until she got to her house, when she turned to the teacher and said, "I'm so happy—that's the first time a boy ever kissed me!" She then raced out of the car and into her house. The next day a physical education instructor, talking to the same teacher in the lunchroom, told her there had been quite a bull session in the boys' shower that morning and that Phillip had been talking about his "making out" with Pat after school the day before, implying very clearly that today would be the day of total conquest. Neither teacher was surprised by this difference in stories; it is the most frequent occurrence in any high school. If you could only believe that almost every other student in your school is as anxious and insecure as you are, then you might also be able to accept the fact that other people lie and boast about their sophisticated adventures—as much as you probably do!

Another problem that arises during these years of self-doubting is that in an effort to please others, you sometimes find yourselves playing very different roles with different people. Andrew, age fifteen, wrote, "The girl who lives on my block is very shy, so when

I'm around her, I am very serious and quiet. The girl I like best in school has a great sense of humor, so when I'm around her I become a clown and I'll do just about anything to try to make her laugh. At home I act like I'm a very serious student and when I'm with a bunch of boys at the bowling alley, I talk like I'm a sex maniac. None of these people is really me, and sometimes I begin to wonder if there *is* a real me."

In trying to fight against this kind of selling out—because sooner or later almost every young person finds that the price is too high—the most natural thing to do is to try to find one or more people with whom you *can* be yourself and be open and honest. After saying that popularity is the most important thing, most teen-agers add, "and also having someone to confide in." The problem is, whom can you really trust? Many of the most intense friendships don't last too long. Suppose you have bared your soul to your best friend, and two months later she is somebody else's best friend? *Nothing terrible is going to happen* as far as these difficulties in friendships are concerned. Yes, some of you will confide in others who may turn out to be less than trustworthy. Some of the most important relationships you ever have will end abruptly. There are gossips, there is often cruelty in places where no one feels really secure. But important things are happening.

Friendships during adolescence are experiments. You are learning a great deal about yourself: what you like and don't like, what people like or don't like about you. Most adults can recall friendships that might have lasted only a few months, but which left deep and lasting impressions. It is a time for testing.

In this process there are many deep wounds. Martha, twelve, wrote, "I had a very dear friend named Sandra. We used to talk every minute we could. Then I began to see that she was always busy. She would never come to see me unless I made a big thing of it. Every day I would try to talk to her and she would read magazines, not noticing me on purpose. Then I found out she had a new best friend. That really hurt me. Sandra and I were best friends since fourth grade. I also worry because I told her my innermost secrets." Gloria, age fourteen, writes, "I liked a boy named Donald. He wasn't good-looking, just a simple guy, and he's really not outstanding in any way. But I liked him a lot. He liked me too—a lot, but then my girl friend, she always used to tell me he was funny looking, she took him away. I don't know for what reason, but he likes her now. My other friends tell me she just wants every boy to like her and then she drops them. I don't want to believe that about my best friend but it's turning out to be true." Rita, age thirteen, writes, "Me and Betty and Leila fight. One time we gang up on Leila. Another time she and Betty gang up on me. We talk behind each other's back. I think all teen-agers have this problem."

Rita is right. And there are very good reasons why friendships can be intense but brief, why cliques are formed, why two friends will make a scapegoat out of a third friend. There are two main reasons for these experiences. The first is that when a person feels insecure it makes him feel more self-confident if he and someone else can gang up on a third person, who becomes the outsider. For a little while, this ganging up makes you feel more secure. The other reason is that you are growing and changing so fast that you need to experiment with new and different relationships as your personality is changing. The challenge is not to feel that you have failed terribly every time a friendship breaks up. It does not mean that you are not a lovable person; what it means is that this particular friendship has been outgrown by one or both of the people involved.

What is really remarkable is that during this period of growth, when so many of you are suffering from such great feelings of self-doubt, you are actually able to develop many fine and helpful relationships with each other. Lillian, age sixteen, writes, "Ruthie and I are close like sisters. She got suspended from school and it fell kind of hard on her because it was the first time. She began to cry and we tried to cheer her up. We succeeded."

As most of you know, one of the places that you get the most help yourself, and are often able to comfort and support a friend, is on the telephone. That is another major arena for fights with parents. On the one hand, the needs and rights of every member of the family must be respected; on the other hand, the telephone is often the very best part of teen-age friendships. There is a logical explanation for this. When you are shy and don't have much self-confidence, when you want someone to tell your troubles to, but you are afraid of getting too close, talking to a friend on the telephone is a way of being very close—but not too close. It is harder, during adolescence, to face another person when you are talking about your most important feelings. What seems often to happen is that both people *do* tend to respect each other's privacy more when they share secret thoughts on the phone than when they meet in person.

Before the telephone was invented, people wrote each other long, very intimate letters, saying things they might never dare to say directly to each other. Young people today feel about the telephone the way their grandparents or great-grandparents felt about writing to each other. A little distance often makes it easier to be oneself.

As much as it may drive other people in the family crazy, it is true that teen-agers can often be kinder to each other, more truly helpful, more natural in a telephone friendship than in an open confrontation. What usually happens is that as you become more self-confident and less shy, you gradually begin to prefer talking directly with each other, but this takes time. Perhaps this is something you can help your parents to understand. It doesn't mean that you can disregard the rights of others, or the expense that is involved, but it may mean that parents will be willing to tolerate more of your long conversations on the phone.

During the adolescent years we tend to choose friends for a variety of reasons—some of which we may not be really aware of. For example, when I was about thirteen years old, I had a friend named Clara. For almost a year we were best friends. I was a fat, studious, shy girl, scared to death of boys. I was very close to my parents and wanted very much to make them proud of me. Clara was considered the sexiest girl in the class. She wore high heels and net stockings, which were considered very daring at that time. She had dates with much older boys, she talked about clothes all the time, and she didn't much care what her parents thought about her lack of good grades. One of my teachers called my mother, she was so worried about this "undesirable friendship." My mother was very smart. She told the teacher not to worry about it. Both my parents made Clara feel very welcome in my house. In later years, as I learned more about myself, I realized that deep inside that good, fat little girl, was a lot of wishing that I could be and act like Clara! We were each like one side of a whole person—two extremes. The teacher was afraid I would become more like Clara; to some degree she was right. But Clara became more like me, too. In fact, we helped each other to become less one-sided. I became more interested in clothes, more confident with boys; Clara became a warmer, more honest person, more interested in learning.

Sometimes we choose a friend because that friend expresses a side of ourselves that we are not yet able to express. Sometimes we may choose a friend who is very much like ourselves. Gerry writes, "The funny thing is that there are some things I can't stand about myself. But my best friend is the same kind of person, and I *like* those things when I see them in her." This kind of friendship often helps you to realize that we only hate certain characteristics in ourselves because we are so unsure of ourselves. By having a friend with the same qualities, we begin to be more objective about our own assets.

Some teen-age friendships are a way of gaining approval and being popular. We may choose a friend simply because other people will be impressed. We are often surprised to discover that these turn out to be very meaningful friendships; the wrong reasons may sometimes lead us to the right person. Some friendships are a way of rebelling against parents and other adults. Glen, age fifteen, said, "For two years I went around with the roughest, toughest kids I could find. I couldn't figure out why I did it—most of the time they scared me. Then I began to realize I was losing interest and I didn't know why. Then I realized my father had stopped yelling at me about going with such bums. Once he stopped yelling, I stopped going with them."

By the time you get to be sixteen, seventeen, and eighteen, friendships will change a great deal. You will find you trust each other more. You will choose each other because you have common interests and ideas. Or it may be that you stimulate each other's minds because you are so different. Friendships begin to be deeper and to last longer; often these are the beginnings of relationships you may have for the rest of your life. In the midst of the more tumultuous years, between twelve and sixteen, it is important to remember that failing in friendships is both necessary and important. Choosing the wrong friends can be as valuable as choosing the right ones. In both cases you are learning and growing and changing through these experiences. Another important thing to remember is that popularity in the early teens has absolutely no relationship to whether or not you will be liked and loved by others when you are older. Some of the quietest violets in your class will become wild and dazzling tiger lilies, while the majority of the people you now envy most will be, ten or more years from now, the very people about whom someone will say, "Whatever happened to . . .?"

To some degree you just have to make up your mind that you will be happy one day and miserable the next; that good and bad friendships will come and go; that you will feel self-conscious and uneasy in many of your relationships. That is just the natural state of things. On the other hand, there is one very important thing you can begin working at which will help right now and make you a nicer person for the rest of your life. It's a very hard thing to do when you are twelve to sixteen years old. But it is worth trying. And that is to stop thinking about yourself when you are with others.

I have never met and talked to any adult, who was reminiscing about the problems of being young, who didn't agree that beginning to try to think how others were feeling was the starting point for losing his or her own self-consciousness. Many of you are hopefully making this discovery.

Anne, age fourteen, wrote: "I am terribly self-conscious because I have to wear braces. It just about kills me. I used to think about it all day in school, and if anybody was friendly, especially a boy, I would wonder, 'Now what's the matter with him, can't he see how ugly I look?' Then a new family moved near us and there was a boy who also wore braces. He was very shy and really homely looking, and I felt very sorry for him. We were on the same school bus, and one day I sat down next to him, just because I felt sorry for him. He turned out to be a very nice person and we became good friends. Feeling sorry for him made me forget my own braces."

One of the most touching true-life stories is the autobiography of Eleanor Roosevelt, in which she tells about how she felt about herself. She had a beautiful mother but she was considered a very homely child. Her mother even teased her about it and called her "Granny." She was a lonely child and very unhappy much of the time. But gradually she discovered that feeling the way she did helped her to understand other people, and that when she showed her sympathy, people were drawn to her. By teaching herself to think and care about others, she became one of the most loved women in the world.

As you gain in self-confidence your goals in friendship will change. Instead of being preoccupied with popularity, you will be more concerned with relationships of mutual compassion and understanding. Peggy, sixteen, said, "I know I want a lot of friends, but I realize I am over just having a bunch of people act like we are really interested in the other person when all we care about is being popular."

With all the difficulties, finding others your own age with whom to share your life matters more than anything else right now. Shelly, age thirteen, wrote, "Lots of parents don't understand that when you are mad at the world and need a friend to talk to, friends are the best people, but instead they say they don't want you on the phone and you can't have company until your room is clean. If you keep your problems inside they will burst the wrong way someday."

Dating, Sex, and Love

The most complicated and difficult part of teen-age friendships is, of course, relationships with the opposite sex. Ben, age fifteen, writes: "I am deeply in love with this girl. I don't know whether she likes me or not. I know I am young to be in love, but I can't think about anything else." Nothing could be more natural. You are trying to figure out who you are and what you are going to become. You are struggling to free yourself from dependency on your family; you are uneasy about the ways in which your body is changing and the new kinds of sexual feelings and fantasies you are beginning to have; you don't know what people will like and won't like about you—and in the middle of all this, you must also begin the slow and steady experimenting, learning, and growing that will

75

someday lead to love, and perhaps to marriage and parenthood. It's a heavy load!

You live in times when there is much confusion and where you are often forced to make choices before you are really ready to make them because no adults tell you exactly what to do. Even when they *do* tell you, it is almost impossible for them to enforce their rules when you spend so much of your time away from home and there is so much less chaperonage of young people.

You are going to be called upon to make many important decisions about your behavior in the next few years. But remember that these are years of discovery and experimentation, not for making final decisions about your future. You simply will not know enough about yourself or have had a wide enough experience in living, loving, and working to make final commitments. The danger is that out of insecurity and a wish for certainty, you may make decisions which are too final.

The most important measure of popularity in the years from twelve to sixteen is very likely to be whether or not you are popular with the opposite sex. Cecile, age thirteen, writes, "I really don't like boys yet, but all my gang has one or two so I have also." It is very hard to fight against this attitude—but it is a good idea to try! If these are the years for discovering who you are and what you want to do with your life as an adult, popularity, as measured by group standards, is not a very helpful approach. I know it is very hard for you to believe this, but the way in which you and your friends measure popularity now has no relationship to how you will feel when you are eighteen or twenty. By that time, hopefully, you will care far more about the quality of your relationships than the quantity; you will have become more selective in your choice of opposite-sex relationships. But that is probably small comfort right now. Janet writes, "In school the girls tease me because I have no dates and never had a real boyfriend even though I am sixteen. I wish I could have a date. My mother would let me go, but nobody asks me. All I want is a nice boy my age to have a date with. All my friends are popular. They talk about boys all the time. They make me feel miserable. The girls pity me and try to tell me what to do but this makes it worse."

People get ready for dating at as wide a variety of ages as everything else that happens in adolescence. In addition, in most cases sexual maturity comes at a pace very different from that of emotional readiness. Where once young people felt that the adult world held them back too much, a young person growing up today feels compelled to begin dating earlier and earlier, and often this is an unnatural burden. Many of you, who anxiously try to pursue the opposite sex on an individual basis, would really far more enjoy being with young people of your own age in group activities with less emphasis on choosing one steady boy or girl friend. Parents and teachers ought to be doing much more than they are doing to help you begin your relationships with group activities—bowling parties, picnics, square dancing, etc. It is extremely hard to begin going steady before you have had an opportunity to know a variety of young people under less intimate circumstances.

What happens is that because of self-consciousness and anxiety, early coupling often becomes too sophisticated. Gloria, fourteen, says, "Instead of getting to be friends there is a war between the sexes, with girls usually wanting to prove they are popular and desirable and boys wanting to prove that they are sexually experienced and the conquerors." Mario, age fifteen, writes, "If you like a girl you want to tell her but you can't because you're afraid and you get embarrassed so you don't. You just go on liking that person until suddenly, Pow! That girl is going with somebody else and you feel your heart is going to break. But you get over it because suddenly you like somebody else."

Feelings are probably more intense than ever before in your life, and few of you recognize the truth of what Mario is saying. You think you will die if a particular boy or girl doesn't fall in love with you, and if things work out the way you want them to, this seems to be the perfect and enduring love, and when it ends you want to die again—until a new love begins.

The greatest anxiety young people have is that they are not attractive. That is a myth that grows out of your period of development when you are so preoccupied with how you are "turning out." Do you really care so much about finding someone who looks like a Barbie or a Ken doll? Well, neither do most of your friends. It is an emphasis strictly related to getting approval from others, and part of maturing is learning that what is on the inside matters more. As Gail, age fifteen, wrote, "I am none too good-looking but I can make do with what I have."

Another issue that comes up over and over again in discussions with young people is parental restrictions on dating. There is no area in which parents seem more unreasonable. Most of your complaints come under the heading of, "They just don't *understand* at all!" Actually, their behavior is more likely to stem from the fact that they understand very well, indeed. They know that your feelings are very strong at this time but that you are also inexperienced; they are worrying about your making some of the mistakes they may feel they made when they were your age. Hard as this may be for you to believe, your parents *do* remember a great deal about what it feels like to be a teen-ager. Sometimes their fears make them behave in ways that are not helpful; they are so anxious that they make rules which are too strict and this makes it difficult for you to be close to them at a time when they might really be quite helpful.

Gina, age fourteen, writes, "My mother is very strict with me and won't let a boy into the house. There is a boy I like a lot who lives close to me. We go around together but my mother doesn't know. I would feel better if she did know, but I'm scared stiff to tell her. This boy takes me to the show every week but my mother thinks it's just girls." Arthur, age sixteen, says, "There's a girl I like a lot, Norma, but her parents treat me as if I was a rapist. The truth is, I'm very shy. We only started holding hands and kissing a few weeks ago. I really don't want to hurt this girl in any way. But when they set an alarm clock, and say she has to be home at nine, and want to know where we are every minute, I begin to feel guilty, even though I know we are not doing anything wrong."

Sometimes the best approach to parents who set up restrictions that make you behave dishonestly or make you feel uncomfortable is a direct and open confrontation. It isn't easy, but it is worth trying. In Arthur's case, he asked his parents to help him. His mother called Norma's mother and said she'd like to talk to her. They sat down over a cup of coffee and Arthur's mother explained the kind of person Arthur was—a shy, intelligent young man, who was not ready himself for any kind of total relationship, including physical intimacy. Together they discussed some reasonable rules that would allow for the friendship, but would not encourage spending all their time together and would not interfere with schoolwork. For the first time, Norma's parents sat down with Arthur and Norma and explained that they felt Norma should become friends with many different boys and that it was too early for her to get deeply involved with one person. Both young people said they agreed, and Norma's parents became less anxious and therefore less strict.

There are times when parents make rules that are really not so dumb! A fourteen-year-old girl asks, "Why do parents say they don't want their daughter to go out with a boy seventeen or eighteen? Even though the guy knows she's a minor and still wants to go out with her. Do you think the parents just don't like the guy? Do you think it's right that they don't allow them to go out? The reason the parents have is that he is hot tempered and he would never settle down, he is too much of a baby, he isn't my type, but we like each other. The parents just don't understand."

At a time when you are trying to break loose from parental restrictions it is hard to be fair. But it is a good idea to try to think a little about some of the things they are saying. Do you like someone just because he or she makes you feel popular and more secure? Did you choose a boy or girl mostly as a form of rebellion against your parents? Do you really trust and like this person? Or do you already have some doubts and misgivings of your own?

Many young people admit that they are glad their parents make some rules about where they may go, what time they have to be home. Joanne, fourteen, said, "I go with a pretty fast crowd and most of the boys are older than me. I skipped two grades when I was in elementary school. They would treat me like a baby if they thought it was me that wanted to go home at a certain time, but when I tell them it's just my mean parents they feel sorry for me!" Ted, fifteen, admitted, "Sometimes I get so mad at my parents watching over me, I feel like running away from home. But then I realize I'm lucky compared to the kids I know whose parents don't know where they are and don't really care."

What lies behind most parental anxiety, of course, is sex—and the problem is that in most cases it is the one subject they cannot bring themselves to discuss with you and that you don't discuss with them. It is certainly on your minds most of the time too, but because there may not be any adults willing to talk to you about it, what you share with each other tends to be mostly lies and misinformation. Nobody is willing to admit their ignorance, everybody is busily boasting of imaginary conquests—and [in the midst of all this] anyone who has ever spoken to a group of young people your age *always* reports on how shocked they are by the misinformation that is going around! Sex is "The Great Mystery," you hear that it is a source of wonder and delight, and you are experiencing feelings of sexual awakening that are both pleasurable and frightening.

It is normal for both boys and girls to have specific fantasies about sex. We used to think that boys were more easily aroused sexually at an earlier age than girls, that their sexual desires in adolescence were more frequent and intense. Now we are beginning to wonder how much of this had to do with how much girls were inhibited by the expectations of adults. It seems to be true now that more girls are becoming aware earlier of sexual feelings.

What is needed most of all is some clarification of the feelings you all have:

One of the many kinds of love that often occurs during adolescence is what we call "crushes" on another person near your own age or perhaps a little older, of the same or the opposite sex. Edward writes, "My problem is this. About two years ago I entered junior high school here and I met a teacher who in the last two years I have become fond of. After knowing this teacher, I have lost all interest in girls my own age. I think about her all the time. There is nothing I wouldn't do for her. I am not sure but I think this teacher likes me somewhat too, a little more than she likes the other students. Do you think it is wrong to be so attached to this person? My love for her is not infatuation—I believe it is true from my heart."

Crushes are perfectly normal. But it is important to understand the difference between such crushes and other kinds of relationships with one's own immediate friends.

A crush is an ideal relationship; because there is a certain natural distance between yourself and the other person, it is possible to have a kind of dream relationship in which everything is perfect and lives up to your highest hopes. There is also no danger of being rejected. These are people whom you admire greatly; they tell you something about your hopes for yourself and the qualities you want to look for in other people. There is nothing the least unnatural or abnormal about having very intense feelings of love for an older person, of either the same sex or the opposite sex. This is a good and natural way to learn about loving before you are ready for direct experiences with your own age group.

Both boys and girls begin to experience some anxieties about homosexuality during adolescence. This is particularly true for boys because society has always allowed girls and women to hug and kiss each other, to show genuine affection openly. When two girls share their miseries and hug each other, they are not likely to think they may be lesbians. We have done great damage to males in our society by giving them the idea that anytime two boys or men show any physical affection for each other, they are homosexuals. This is not so. In many other countries in the world, grown men kiss and hug each other. In our country we have developed a strange philosophy; if two males really want to show their affection for each other, by putting an arm around each other, they are sissies. But if they get out on a football field and beat each other up, touching each other a great deal in the process, that's being masculine. It is too bad when tenderness is suspect but violence is not.

These attitudes are beginning to change. Young men and women tend to be much less concerned with arbitrary ideas about masculinity and femininity. Men feel free to hug each other when they feel like it; women feel free to be more dominating and ambitious and still enjoy being female. There is a greater naturalness developing between the sexes and less concern about playing rigid and inflexible roles.

A question many young people want to ask about, but are embarrassed to discuss, is masturbation. Masturbation is not harmful in any way. It is a natural way to begin to explore your own sexual feelings. It is the way most people begin their active sexual lives. It becomes a problem only when it is the whole focus of one's attention, to the exclusion of all other interests and activities, or when it occurs at inappropriate places—other than in the privacy of one's own room. It is normal during adolescence to experience sexual fantasies and to release sexual drives through masturbation.

Perhaps the most important subject that concerns you is whether or not to have sexual relations before you are engaged or married. Paula, age twelve, writes, "I think I'm old enough to know more about sex but my mother says I'm too young. As a result I pick up things here and there and am never sure what's true. At the library they keep sex books locked up for adults. How are we supposed to learn anything?" This is really very sad but true: the majority of young people do not get the information and guidance they would really like to get from adults. You have to remember that just one or two generations ago, *nobody* talked to young people about sex. That picture is certainly changing, but it is taking too long, considering the amount of stimulation, freedom, and misinformation you are exposed to. More and more high schools are introducing courses in sex education. Most school and public libraries do have a special section of sex education books for young people, and librarians are now more often trained to help you find the information you are looking for. Here is a brief list* of books that give sound and helpful information; you and a

* Recommended by the Education Department of the Nassau County Mental Health Association.

group of your friends could buy them together if you cannot get them at the library:

How Life Begins by Jules Power. Simon and Schuster, 1965.

Human Growth: The Story of How Life Begins and Goes On by Lester Beck. Harcourt Brace Jovanovich, 1949.

The Human Story—Facts on Birth, Growth and Reproduction by Sadie Hofstein. Lothrop, Lee and Shepard, 1969.

Finding Yourself by Marion Lerrigo and Helen Southard. Available from the American Medical Association, 535 N. Dearborn St., Chicago, IL, 60610, 1970.

Love and Sex In Plain Language by Eric Johnson. J.B. Lippincott, 1967.

Sex Before Twenty: New Answers for Youth by Helen Southard. E.P. Dutton, 1967.

Part of your important decisions about sexual relations ought to include information about the very real hazards of venereal disease. Here are two books written especially for young people on this subject:

V.D.—Venereal Disease and What You Should Do About It by Eric Johnson. J.B. Lippincott, 1973.

VD—The Silent Epidemic by Margaret Hyde. McGraw-Hill, 1973.

It is very important to have accurate information at a time in your life when you will have to make many crucial decisions. Even if you would rather die than admit your feelings of fear, shame, guilt, and ignorance to anyone else, it is helpful if you can admit them to yourself—and do something about them. In addition to the books I've mentioned, I cannot imagine that

somewhere in your life there isn't someone knowl-
edgeable and mature who can tell you what you want
and need to know. A neighbor, an aunt or uncle, an
older cousin, a doctor, a minister, a favorite teacher, a
school nurse or guidance counselor, a married brother
or sister—look around you.

Renee says, "I'm fourteen and if I mention about
boys to my mother, she starts telling me how old she
was before she even looked at a boy. She's always
telling me boys are dangerous." Sometimes when parents make such statements without offering any open-
ings for a real discussion, their children not only become more curious, but the young people may begin
to feel that one way to show how grown up and independent they are is to defy parental warnings and
rules about dating and sex.

Young people have mixed feelings about talking to
parents about sex. On the one hand Margaret, fifteen,
says, "My mother isn't a mother to me. I can't ask any
personal questions. She's just like an outsider to me."
Obviously she wishes she could talk confidentially to
her mother. On the other hand, many young people
agreed with Joseph's attitude, "My parents are *the
last people on earth* that I would ever talk to about
girls and stuff like that. How can you discuss that
with people who will always think about you like
you're still two years old?"

Some parents and teen-agers do manage to talk to
each other; not always so easily or comfortably, but
they do find ways of sharing their ideas. Sometimes it
helps if the discussion is sort of impersonal. Janet, age

fifteen, wrote, "I ask my parents general questions about growing up—about any kid, not me especially, and that makes them more comfortable and me too." Robert, age fourteen, reports, "My parents are from the old school. They were born in Europe and I know they couldn't talk to me about things like sex. But they are very educated people and I know they would worry about me, so I asked my father if he would mind getting me a good book. He said, 'Sure,' and you should have seen the look of relief on his face!"

Some of you have already had sexual experiences, and I also know that others of you may before you marry. Because you are very young, many of these experiences have been or will be upsetting, frightening, and disappointing. Some may have been or will be pleasurable. All will have some element of guilt and anxiety because sexual intercourse among teenagers is still not condoned openly and because pregnancy and venereal disease are very real hazards.

You probably do not believe it when adults tell you that sex can be a meaningful and satisfying experience *only* when you are in love and married. It is true that the deepest joy a man and a woman can share is when they have made a genuine commitment to each other, though lesser relationships may be pleasureable. However, no matter how early you may have developed sexually in terms of physical readiness, the large majority of you are not ready for sexual relationships now. *Physical readiness, alone, is not enough.* Psychological and social readiness are equally important. The question you need to ask yourself is: What happens afterwards? What about the feelings and worries that follow sexual intimacy? If you are mixed up in your inner feelings about yourself at this age, what happens when you add another person's feelings and needs to that load? Are you in any way prepared, on your own, to handle the emotional part of the relationship? On your own, could you handle a pregnancy or venereal disease, now so rampant among young people?

The problem with sexual relationships during a period of complicated growing is that sometimes one gets involved for the wrong reasons. Belinda, age sixteen, writes, "My problem is I go through months or weeks where I want a baby around. I love them so much sometimes I don't care what kind of trouble I get into. Like when I'm on the street or shopping and I see a baby I want to get him or her and run away with it. I baby-sit sometimes like for a week or so but when the parents come home I don't want to leave it. I'm really afraid of getting into trouble with a guy."

Belinda is lucky in that she knows what she is feeling. Sometimes when a young person does not feel loved enough, having a boyfriend or having a baby occurs not because one is truly ready for the experience but is desperately searching for love.

When love comes—or parenthood for that matter —it ought to be from the strength and joy of mature readiness; it ought to be for positive reasons, for happy reasons. When young people get involved in relationships because of feelings of deprivation and unhappiness it can only lead to more of the same.

A teacher told me, "There are a couple of students in my class who I know are having sex relations. The saddest thing about it is that while they can relate to each other physically, they cannot even really *talk* to each other; they don't know each other, they can't express their feelings." Glenda writes, "I was afraid I would lose Ricky if I didn't have sex with him. It's very quick and sort of mechanical, and I was very hurt and disappointed. I am also scared if anyone finds out. In my dreams I think of Ricky and me going to the beach for a long walk, holding hands. Or sometimes I imagine us rowing on a lake and having a picnic together on a little island, with trees. Or sometimes I imagine we go to an amusement park and Ricky wins a big panda for me, shooting at a target. But nothing like that really happens. We go to the drive-in and make out, and he hardly says anything, and then we go home, and I cry until I fall asleep."

The more mature you become the more you will want to make choices for yourself very seriously and carefully. You will want to ask yourself a lot of questions first: "Am I really ready? Will I be afraid? Will it make me worry afterward? Will it hurt this other person whom I really care about?"

When sex is a mechanical act, without wanting to or being able to take responsibility or care for the other person, we rob ourselves of the experience of a different kind of sex, in which it is the end result of getting to know and truly care about another human being. Sex just to feel big, sex to boast about, sex just to get the problem of virginity over and done with is almost never very satisfying.

Most of you are told by parents and teachers that sex before marriage—and certainly before one is at least eighteen—is sinful and dangerous. Yet you know that some of the people you know don't believe these ideas. Kim, age fifteen, asks, "Are my friends bad or are my parents old-fashioned?" It is normal to have strong sexual feelings. It is normal to feel uneasy about what sex is really like. It is also normal for first experiments in sex to be disappointing. This is truer the younger and more inexperienced the person, and where the relationship between the two people is superficial. So it is also normal—and wise—to consider postponing sexual intimacy until one can have a more deeply meaningful relationship. Sexual intercourse does not improve simply by having more and more experiences. The most important ingredient of increased satisfaction is emotional maturity and a more loving relationship with another person.

Sometimes young people themselves can help each other to discover what they are ready for, not what will impress others. Rosalind, age fifteen, writes, "My boyfriend and I broke up a month ago. He told me he was going to find somebody else if I didn't have sex with him. I told him to go ahead. I thought he wasn't going to do it but he did. He still calls me. He's not happy and neither am I." Postponement of full intimacy can often be a sign of maturity.

It is usually still up to the girl to make the final decision about sex relations since the possible conse-

91

quences tend to fall more heavily upon her. Rita, age sixteen, wrote, "I've been going with a boy I like very much. At first we just kissed and hugged a lot but now he wants to make out. So far I don't feel like it, to tell you the truth, but I don't want to lose him." Between not feeling ready and fear of losing a boyfriend, what decision do you think you would make? Is fear of losing someone's attention enough to push you into a relationship for which you are not ready? It shouldn't be. Such relationships almost always end in heartache for both boy and girl, whether they are able to admit it to each other or not.

Even while speaking of some of the dangers and problems, there is *nothing*, but NOTHING, that can happen to you which is the end of the world! No matter how big your mistakes, no matter how terrible it seems at the moment, *it will pass* and, hopefully, you will learn something from the experience. A few years ago I interviewed a number of young women who were being forced to marry by their parents when it was discovered they were pregnant. When they were found out, all of them thought their lives were over. A few years later, they were remarkably wise and mature. Some of the marriages had worked out, some had not. Some of the young women were divorced, some had stayed married and had other children, a few had decided just before the planned wedding to give the child up for adoption or to have an abortion. No matter how parents may react, no matter how much guilt and shame you experience at the time, you can use such an experience for learning more about yourself. The fact that you have gotten yourself into difficulty may tell you that you have not valued your own self enough and that you need to find someone who can help you see why you have had such a poor opinion of yourself. The reason that a "catastrophe" sometimes turns into something positive is that finally you and the adults in your life face the fact that you are in trouble, and you begin to get the counseling, the help you need.

While girls are likely to be catapulted into too early sex by a desire to be popular, boys feel compelled, sometimes too soon, by a need to prove their masculinity; "real he-men keep making out." That is not true, no matter what the boys in your age group may think about the matter. What girls—and women —end up admiring and valuing most in a man when they themselves are more mature is gentleness, caring, a man who concerns himself with being loving as well as sensual. And grown men discover that they feel most masculine of all when loving concern for another human being is an important ingredient of a sexual relationship. Unfortunately at thirteen, fourteen, and fifteen, boys are more afraid of being laughed at and girls are more afraid of being alone than probably they ever will be again, and it is these feelings that too often make the decision rather than a thoughtful person making choices based on real needs.

These are the years for beginning to develop the ability to really think for oneself, to make decisions about one's present and future life. Your life is valuable—you are a precious person. You will love and be loved if you begin now to fulfill all the possibilities that are in you. These are the years to test and experiment with a variety of friendships. The world is really not lost and your life is really not over when these relationships are painful and end in failure. It is one of the best ways to learn. And you are just at the threshold of what loving can really mean: caring about someone else as much as or more than yourself.

7

Caring for Your Life: Drugs, Alcohol, and Other Troubles

Adolescence is a time when young people tend to be daring, to be eager to take chances. It is a time for adventure and excitement. It is also a time when one is most easily influenced by other people because of insecurity and lack of self-confidence. A psychologist discussing the use of drugs among teen-agers said, "The *real* addiction, when one is young, is wanting approval from other kids!"

You have probably discovered that you can be several different people. You behave one way when you are alone, another way when you are with one or two others, and completely differently when you are with a larger group. Most of the potentially dangerous or destructive things you may try occur when you are with larger groups. Ramon, age fifteen, says, "I am usually a quiet person when I am alone. I am what you might call a worrier. But sometimes when I am with a group of boys my age, I can't tell what I might do. Sometimes I get very funny and I like it when they laugh. I get crazier and crazier the more they laugh. Once they dared me to jump from one apartment house roof to the next and I did it. Later I got the shakes. I could have gotten killed."

Groups can be dangerous. The combination of many personalities together seems to take on a personality of its own and the group becomes like another person. Young people will get drunk on alcohol, smoke pot, experiment with hard drugs, drive faster, and do more daring feats with others than they would ever consider for one moment if they were alone. It is therefore very important that when you are in a group you try to think about what you are doing; are you doing things you would *not* do if you were alone? If the answer is yes, it may be time to think twice.

The highest rate of drug addiction, committing crimes, and car accidents occur during the teen years. Partly it has to do with the new character taken on by a group. This is reinforced by each member of the group wanting to belong. Partly it is due to youthful vitality and inexperience—a conviction that one can do anything and survive, and this leads to taking chances. This is true of every generation of young people, but in recent years the chances have become greater and the consequences more serious. Young people have always been daring, but what happens to them depends in part on what is available to them.

One hundred years ago, if you lived in a small town or a rural area, a group of teen-age boys would probably have gone to the apple orchard of some crotchety farmer they didn't like and stolen some of his apples. He would have reported this to their families, and the families would have meted out some form of punishment, but most people would have said, "Boys will be boys," and nothing much would have happened. Fifty years ago kids were smoking cigarettes in the balconies of movie theaters or singing in the city streets at two in the morning while people yelled at them from the windows. Getting drunk on alcohol was the most common way of altering reality and lowering inhibitions. Some young people also smoked pot experimentally through the generations, but not on a massive scale until the 1960s.

The times we live in now are much more complex. More people are hurting; life has become far more difficult. There is less tolerance of youthful playfulness, and a young person can be picked up by the police just for loitering. As towns turned into cities and cities into overpopulated nightmares of dirt and noise and too many people and slums, individual families could no longer assume full responsibility for themselves, and the police began to be called on to handle such situations. Young people have more contact with police today than ever before in the history of this country.

It is a time when many adults are unhappy, confused, and frightened. In such an environment there are also a great many young people for whom life is full of pain. If life is not actually terrifying, the days may seem all gray and boring.

Sal reports, "Half the kids on drugs don't have fathers at home and their mothers raise hell with their kids and they don't know what's going on. They get caught stealing out of a store, and when the police call their home and ask for their mother or father, there is no one there to help." Certainly those who become addicted to heroin or other drugs tend to be young people who are deeply unhappy; the person they hate most in all the world is themselves. From early childhood they have gotten the feeling that nobody cares whether they are alive or dead, and they learn not to care too much themselves. Until the whole country begins to show deep concern for such unhappy young people, we will not be able to offer the kind of help that is needed to solve these problems. But there is beginning to be a change. Most cities are beginning to try to develop a variety of programs of rehabilitation, and if these help, it is because they focus attention on helping an individual to value his or her own life, to begin to take responsibility for one's welfare, and to have personal pride in what one can do for oneself.

The problems of drugs and alcohol (fast becoming equally serious) are not, however, only problems for people who live in poverty or people who feel rejected by society. As you all know, there are drug pushers and drug addicts in the most well-to-do suburbs. This is a very hard time to be growing up in America, and fears about oneself and the future have hit young people, wherever they live. However, drugs or alcohol will not help us solve any of our problems. Instead they create serious hazards.

It is true that there is a great deal we still do not know about drugs such as LSD. We *do* know that LSD can cause emotional turmoil leading to suicide. We also know that amphetamines ("uppers" or "speed") can do permanent damage to the brain. We also know that because traffic in drugs is illegal, there is an ever-present danger that what one is buying may be contaminated or even poisonous.

Any chemical means of escaping from painful realities can have serious consequences. It is very important that you be well informed about the reasons you may be searching for such experiences, as well as current knowledge and research findings about the effects of marijuana, heroin, amphetamines, LSD, and alcohol on your mind and body. Here are two books written especially for young people, which you can buy or borrow from a public or school library:

Drug Abuse and Addiction: A Fact Book for Parents and Teen-Agers and Young Adults by Barbara Milbauer. Crown, 1970.
Alcohol: Our Biggest Drug Problem by Joel Fort. McGraw-Hill, 1973.

Parents and teachers are often as confused and scared as the young people themselves. Carrie writes, "Some parents catch their kids with a cigarette when they are fourteen, and tell you that you'll be a big Dope Addict by the time you're sixteen." Due to the very harsh and punitive controls by the Federal Narcotics Bureau, the entrance of organized crime into the sale of drugs, and the general confusion among both scientists and laymen about various kinds of hallucinogens, people often behave quite hysterically.

Hard drugs like the amphetamines, which may actually damage the brain, and heroin must be brought under control. I would hope that this would be medical control because those who use such drugs have psychological and environmental problems and need help, not punishment. Lenny, sixteen, writes: "As far as grass is concerned, it seems to me that most of the laws are designed to punish the young and the poor. Grass is now smoked in moderation by vast numbers of adults in this country. Many of them are lawyers, doctors, teachers, businessmen—very respectable middle-aged people. Almost none of them are caught or convicted or sent to prison. At the same time, any young person knows he may be searched at any moment and that the likelihood of imprisonment is very great if he is found possessing marijuana."

But, having said that, what comes next? However unjust the laws may seem to you, who will suffer in the long run by breaking them? You have to ask yourself whether the risk is worth the possible temporary pleasure. And if smoking pot is worth the risk, then it may suggest that real life is not as full of excitement and color as it might be, and maybe it is time to think about how you can feel high without chemicals.

Lena, age sixteen, writes, "I used to feel bored and very restless most of the time. I felt I could never feel good unless I was high on grass or getting drunk on beer. Then last summer I got a job through the Youth Corps, working with a bunch of kids in a recreation center. There was this man there, a young guy, he was the director of the place. He had a great sense of humor, he could make me laugh anytime. We took these little kids on trips to the country and all over, and this man, he really liked me, and he turned me on to really seeing things around me, and he told me getting those kids to love me was better than the best high. He was right. My life is different now. Just thinking about the places we went and him liking me, and showing me how to look at things like flowers and sunsets, and walking in puddles with these little kids after the rain—he turned me on to different things."

Whether you are talking about addictive drugs, or marijuana, or the dangers of smoking two packs of cigarettes a day, or getting VD, or an unwanted pregnancy, or a serious car accident due to speeding, or getting caught for stealing—every one of these activities means that you are taking chances with your life. The more dangerous the activity, the less you value that life. Floyd, age sixteen, had an interesting way of looking at it. He said, "You got to think of yourself like a car that has to make a long trip. If you keep it in good condition and work on it, and give it a lot of loving attention, you can figure on having a long, good trip. If you treat it lousy, you won't get no place."

When it comes right down to it, you are the only

person who can care enough about yourself to give yourself the very best. You can cheat yourself of your future, or you can give your future "a lot of loving attention." Others can help—and your task right now is to search for those people who will help you value yourself—but the final decision is yours. What do you want: a search for more adventures in the real world and self-fulfillment through using your own talents, or a short dive into momentary thrills and unusual sensations that cannot last and that leave you more full of pain and discouragement than you were before?

Freda, age fifteen, wrote, "I'm a homegirl. My friends want me to look for boys and smoke weed and have babies. I say no, I want to protect myself for better things." Only people with personal dignity and pride can make such choices. That means that the central task is to begin to believe your life matters. I believe it, and I know there are others you can find to help you believe it.

The Most Important Question:
Who Am I?

In the very beginning of this book I said that adolescence was the hardest time of life. I still believe that! But it is time to add another sentence: The most wonderful things can happen during and after that struggle to leave childhood behind.

I started this book with a poem by Angela Powlen. She wrote another poem a year or more later:

> Sometimes I don't know who I am
> Or what I feel
> Or what I like
> Or what I want
> I do things that upset me
> I eat things I don't like
> I say things that I don't even know what they mean
> And tell people I like them when I know darn well
>   I hate them

And I tell people who I love that I hate them and
    wish they'd go away even though I know that I
    want them with me.
But sometimes I'm me
I do things I like
Say things that mean something
I'm with people I like and know how I feel
And usually when I'm that way I feel good!

It seems to me that in this poem Angela has moved beyond just describing the feelings of adolescence. She is beginning to work at figuring at who she really is, and as she says herself, the more she does that, the better she feels.

Finding out who you are, what you want to do with your life, discovering your uniqueness—what makes you the special person you are, different from anyone else in the world—this is the most exciting task anyone can work at.

It takes great courage to begin that journey into selfhood. Janet, age fourteen, wrote, "I have got to teach myself how to be human. It should be like I'm satisfied with me and those who like it, fine, and those who don't, fine. They don't have to be bothered with me. I want to be confident enough to be able to say that."

Think back to a time when you really felt very good about yourself and began to have some hopeful feelings about your future. When a ninth-grade class was asked to do this, here are some of the answers they gave:

"One time my two best friends were talking about a kid in our class who was real dumb. They were making fun of her. I said I wouldn't listen and I went home. I was shaking because I was afraid they would turn on me, too, but I felt proud of myself."

"The high school I go to—they make you take art classes. I never did much in that area, I always thought it was more like for girls. There was this real great teacher, I really liked him a lot and I began sketching and painting and he said I had a lot of talent and should major in art. I really enjoyed it, but when I told my parents what the teacher said they laughed and my Dad said that was sissy stuff. I really felt very bad after that. I didn't take any the second year of high school and I felt really bad about it. I felt lousy about everything, to tell the truth. Now I'm a junior and I decided I want to try to do what I like and that's drawing. This teacher has been telling me about commercial art schools, and I don't talk about it at home, but for the first time I think a lot about what I'll do in the future and I get really excited."

"If there is one thing I can't stand it is Hard Rock. But you're supposed to love it and I put on a good act because that's all the kids in school listen to. Yesterday for the first time, I said I hated it, in front of two boys I like a lot. They looked at me as if I was a worm, and I expected to feel terrible, and they'd really put me down. But then another boy said, 'I like a girl to have a mind of her own.' I never even noticed him before. Now I think I like him better than the other two."

Nothing is more important now than trying to find out who you really are and what it means to become more truly your "real self," rather than trying to live up to the image or expectations other people have of you. Adolescence is a turning point in your life, and if you can begin to think seriously about who you are and what you want to do with your life, it can and does influence all the years ahead of you.

It is natural that the first image you had of yourself was one that you got from your parents. You were tiny and completely dependent, and you wanted them to love you as much as you loved them. You believed whatever they told you about yourself because you had no knowledge or experience to judge for yourself.

Try to think for a minute: what picture do you have of yourself that reflects your parents' ideas?

Gail, sixteen, says: "I guess I think of myself as sort of blah. Not much personality. I think my parents feel that I am kind of dumb but sweet, and as soon as I get out of high school I'll be a supermarket clerk or something like that, and get married and have children. I sometimes think this is true and other times I think I would rather die than have such an ordinary life."

And Henry, fifteen, says: "There is no question about what my parents and I think about me. They think I'm bad. I've been in trouble with them since I was born! I am a very excitable person, and I get mad very easy. I can't stand sitting still—I got to be going all the time—I'm a very restless person. I have always been sorry that I was such a mess and made my parents so disappointed in me."

Each of us is born with our own special differences.

Some of us are quite serene and easygoing, some restless and discontented. Each of our parents has likes and dislikes; they get along better with some people than with others; and they have memories of their own childhood and what their own parents liked and didn't like. A lot of the attitudes you developed about yourself had to do with these factors over which neither you nor your parents had much control. If you happened to have the looks and personality of your Aunt Grace, your mother's older sister, who drove your mother crazy when she was little, it is possible that you might develop the attitude about yourself that you are a bossy, difficult person to live with. Or if you were born to be a little shy and retiring, if you enjoy reading and listening to music, and your father (after waiting for a son after having three girls) expected you to play baseball with him and become a great athlete, then you might have a pretty low opinion of people like yourself who are not good at sports. When we are very little we want desperately to please our parents, and we often sell out; we decide to try to be what they want us to be instead of ourselves.

Maggie has a tough competitive spirit and a well-coordinated body; when she was very young, she wanted to climb and run; when she was older, she wanted to learn to swim and sail, then ski and skate. But her mother always wanted her to play with dolls and wear cute little feminine dresses, and her father wanted her to be "Daddy's little sweetheart." Maggie tries to be what they want, and wonders why she is so unhappy—until, toward the end of high school, she

107

gets enough encouragement from teachers and friends to try out for the girls' hockey team. The whole world changes as she begins to do what comes naturally, not what is expected.

The image that you have had of what you are really like is too often the image reflected in your parents' eyes. This is the time of life to look at yourself with your own eyes. That is not an easy thing to do. It means you have to begin to go on a great exploration, you have to become more consciously aware of what you like and don't like, what makes you feel a sense of joy and what you hate doing, what you do with ease and pleasure and what tasks give you a headache or a stomachache.

The difficulty is that as you begin to move away from the attitudes of your family, you need and want to feel well liked by your friends, and what usually happens is that, for a time at least, you accept what you think your friends think of you and want you to be. Maybe you really want to wear frilly and feminine clothes, but you wear jeans and floppy shirts because that's the style; maybe you are fascinated by chemistry and physics and would like to spend most of your time studying, reading, doing experiments, but your friends laugh at "long-hair intellectuals" and so you go bowling. To some degree this is a necessary part of growing up. But as you begin to feel more self-confident, you have to discover and be who you really are, not what your parents think you are or want you to be, not what your friends think you are or want you to be.

108

This means that some of the time you have to be alone. You probably don't like that idea any more than you like the idea of being different. But in order to get in touch with your own feelings, you need to be alone with your own thoughts. At first this might be for a half-hour, then maybe for a whole afternoon, and then maybe for a whole day once in a while. Sometimes the best way to start knowing more about yourself is to think about what you like to do best and then do it alone. It might be walking through some part of a city, in the woods, or along a beach. It might be going to a movie or it might be sitting alone in your room, listening to music. It might be going fishing or lying in a hammock looking at the sky. Too many teachers and parents tend to act as if you are doing nothing when you are doing nothing. Being alone, just dreaming and letting your mind wander, is really doing something very important. It is a time when you are getting to know yourself better, and you have a right to ask to be allowed to spend some time in this way. When we keep ourselves busy doing things every minute, we rarely have time for thinking and feeling, and too many adults have lost touch with themselves because they think that important things only happen when you are busy.

When you are twelve, thirteen, and fourteen, it is a good idea not to try to make too many plans or too many decisions about the future. These are years in which you need to have a wide variety of experiences. But as you approach fifteen and sixteen, you can probably go further along the road to finding out more about yourself if you begin to make some decisions. That doesn't mean that any of your plans should be final. The longer you take before making up your mind about your future work, the more likelihood that you will enjoy what you do. Too many young people have felt so uncertain and so insecure that they have made a quick decision about what they want to do—and then they are stuck with it. You will be growing and changing for many more years and no decision should be final about anything.

But you can begin to test yourself. And one of the best ways to do this is to work. By the middle of high school it would be good if every student had to do some kind of volunteer work for which he or she would get school credit. Some schools are beginning to do this, but whether yours does or not, you might think about doing it on your own. It will certainly be a helpful addition to your school record later on when you go on to college or begin working.

Mary Ellen, age fifteen, is an only child, and she's always been interested in little children. One afternoon a week she works as a volunteer in a day care center. She's having such a good time that she's thinking of a career as a nursery school teacher. Jay, age sixteen, had to earn his own spending money. He's had four or five after-school jobs, trying out different things to see what he seems to like the most. His job is almost always sweeping and cleaning, but he's meeting people in different fields of work, asking questions, and listening. So far he has worked on Saturdays for a lawyer, mowing his lawn and washing windows. The lawyer was very friendly and they talked quite a lot. He has also worked in a pharmacy, and he's sure he'd hate filling prescriptions all day. He has worked in a supermarket and as he looked and listened, it seemed to him that the manager of the store had a very interesting life. Vivian, age fifteen, has a younger sister with a seriously crippling disease, and she thinks she might be interested in working with handicapped children someday. She works as a volunteer in the children's ward at the hospital one afternoon a week. Bert, age sixteen, was hoping to get a job as an assistant camp counselor but he had never been around school-age children much, so he decided to try it out by working at a community center that had after-school recreation for children whose mothers were working. He found out he couldn't stand being with little kids and so he gave up the idea of working in a camp as a counselor. He said, "I'd rather wash dishes all summer in a restaurant than have to run after kids!" He has learned something about himself—at least as he is right now. Two years from now he may feel differently.

Some kind of work experience is important for another reason too: it helps to build the self-confidence which in turn helps a person make his own decisions. There are many people who learn more through doing than they do sitting in a class listening. Michael, age sixteen, reported, "I think I have felt dumb in school since about third grade. I also got bored a lot. This past summer I got a job at a gas station and even though I was hired to just sell gas I hung around the mechanic and watched what he was doing. After a while, he began to teach me about cars and I really got very interested. By the end of the summer he was letting me work with him, and I found out I'm not so dumb, I just prefer working with my hands on machinery instead of trying to learn from books."

Self-confidence also comes from feeling that you are useful and that you can help other people. In some schools the high school students are now being encouraged to help teach reading to the children in first and second grade. Wherever this has been tried it has worked out beautifully, especially where the high school student has had trouble with reading and writing himself. Young children seem to learn more easily from someone who understands just how they feel—how confused and anxious they are about learning. And young people who feel unsure of themselves gain in feelings of pride and self-respect when they realize how much they can help someone else. Even if your school doesn't yet have such a program, you might talk to your adviser about doing this on your own. There are so many serious problems in every community—so many things that need the help of concerned people.

In one church in Harlem, the minister developed a program of rehabilitating run-down old tenements. A community group was formed and, with the help of the city, got some money to finance rehabilitation work after which the current tenants would be allowed to buy their own apartments at very low cost and form a cooperative. The minister said, "One of the most exciting and rewarding parts of this project was the work that was done by high school students in the neighborhood school. Every Saturday a group of volunteers helped with painting, floor scraping, plastering, and general carpentry. I have never seen such enthusiasm and such high spirits among young people. And they could be justly proud of the real contribution they were making. I think they were learning more . . . that one day a week than the five days they were spending in school."

Sometimes the best way to deal with your anxieties and uncertainties is to get so involved in the problems of other people that there is no time to think about yourself. Not all the time, for we need to deal with our own problems, but part of the time. Success in helping others provides us with feelings of pride and fulfillment. It is important at all stages of life to feel needed.

You have more natural vitality and energy than at any other time of life. You are also full of hopes and dreams. This is the time for high ideals and the wish to help make the world a better place in which to live. Whatever task you set yourself to fulfill your hopes for the world's future will make you feel good about yourself, whether it is volunteering to lick envelopes for the election of a political leader, or helping to clean up the garbage in a vacant lot so some kids can play baseball, or writing for the school magazine. One way to find yourself is to care a great deal about the welfare of others.

There is a place you can begin to make decisions

about your own life no matter what is happening at school or at home, and that is inside your own head. It is a private place that really belongs to you, alone, and you can dream your own dreams and experiment with different kinds of future plans. That "headwork" is just as valuable and important as anything you are actually doing. Finding out who you are is not a search that ever has any final answers. You are changing all the time; and to have the richest life, growth and change should always be happening, whether you are thirteen or sixty.

Parents and teachers tend too often to force you to think about your future when what is important is right now. It is important to savor the moment you are living, without always worrying about the future. To some degree at least, you can tell yourself, no matter what others may tell you, that you need to take it slow and easy and not rush or push yourself. You need to make room in your life for lots of mistakes. We can learn more, usually, from our mistakes than from anything else—if we use our mistakes for a lot of careful thinking about what went wrong and why. People who grow the most, who learn to use their gifts to the fullest degree, are almost always people who can tolerate a great deal of uncertainty. They don't have to have final answers all the time; they are willing to experiment, take reasonable chances, accept blunders, and go on from there.

Try to remember the times in the past year or so when you have learned a great deal about yourself and how you really feel. Chances are these experiences were not very comfortable or easy. Renee writes that she remembers best the time she lied to her parents about driving in a car with some pretty wild friends. They had told her she was not to go, but she went anyway. She was never so scared in her life, and while no one ever caught her in the lie, she learned that she is not about to endanger her life again. Or there was the time that Mark decided he just had to try heroin because he'd heard so much about it and was so curious. He had a bad time but he learned something very important; he wanted to use his brain for more important things.

Even very serious mistakes are not the end of the world. Patty got pregnant at the age of fifteen. She had to tell her parents and wished she could just kill herself. Her parents and her doctor and she agreed that she was much too young to go through a pregnancy, much less become a mother, and so she had an abortion. Her feelings of shame and guilt and remorse were so overwhelming that she felt her life could never be worthwhile or happy again. What she realized a year or two later was that she had learned a great deal about herself and that her life was far from over. She said, "My parents and I had never talked about sex or love or anything like that. I am the only child and they own a small grocery store where they work about eighteen hours a day. I was alone a lot and very lonely. I found out I was angry too, that they left me alone so much. I wanted somebody to pay a lot of attention and love me, and even though I was scared to death, I began going out with an eighteen-year-old boy who lived in our apartment build-ing. I wanted to be close to somebody, and I was glad somebody wanted to be with me. He told me we would get married when I was sixteen. Well, when I found out I was pregnant, the first person I confided in was the nurse at school. She's a wonderful woman and I knew her quite well. She helped me tell my parents and when they almost killed me, she made them understand I needed help. I have been seeing a psychologist at the mental health clinic, and I guess in a way this whole experience has saved my life. I understand I was looking for love and approval at the wrong time and in the wrong place. I feel that no matter what happens to me, no matter how awful, I'll be able to be all right. I guess you could say I grew up."

Even though Patty learned from her experience, it was self-destructive to begin with; it was hurtful to herself and everyone who cared about her. The goal of self-understanding and self-discovery is to respect yourself so much that you can begin to make more thoughtful and careful decisions that will help you to grow well. That is really the heart of the matter; dis-covering what a fine and good person you really are— that you are worthy of self-respect as well as the re-spect and love of other people.

In the long run, each of us needs to be loved more than anything else in the world. We need friends and family. We need to live in a world with people who really matter to us. But the beginning of this must be caring about ourselves. When we really feel good about being ourselves, then we are ready to choose who will be the other necessary and important people in our lives.

Every single human being is a precious person. The struggles you are now going through to grow up are painful and difficult but they are also exciting and important. You are experiencing a great adventure in finding out who you are and what you want to be and do with your own life. When you are struggling the hardest, that is the time to remember that your life is valuable and sacred. As one young person put it, "There is a singing in me in spite of the pain."